* * *
ESSENTIAL

[powertools]

19

tools to renovate and repair your home

[contents]

FIRST EDITION
ISBN 0-9666753-1-2

10 9 8 7 6 5 4 3 2

COVER PHOTOGRAPHY:
JIM COOPER

Library of Congress Cataloging-in-Publication Data
This Old House essential power tools: 19 essential tools to renovate
and repair your home. -- 1st ed.
           p.   cm.
        ISBN 0-9666753-1-2 (alk. paper)
        1. Power tools.   I. This Old House magazine.
TJ1195. T52   1998   98-41968
643' .7—dc21

WHAT if a circular saw HAD ROSEWOOD GRIPS? WOULD IT WORK BETTER? WHEN IT COMES TO CHOOSING TOOLS, BUYING what you don't NEED

—OR WORSE, NOT BUYING WHAT YOU DO NEED—FREQUENTLY RESULTS in projects that don't go quite right. If you've ever wondered how to choose the right power tool for the kind of work you're doing, find out from a couple of *This Old House* pros: master carpenter Norm Abram and contractor Tom Silva. Norm and Tom learned to renovate and repair houses in an era barely removed from total reliance on hand tools, and they bring that tradition of painstaking craftsmanship to their use—and choice—of power tools. The work that goes into building or remodeling a house is faster and louder than it used to be, and not necessarily better for all that. But it's not necessarily worse, either: Anyone who worships only hand tools ought to hand-drill 30 holes into concrete sometime. *** The birth of a house hasn't always been accompanied by the wailing of saws and the syncopated *pop, pop-pop* of nail guns. In fact, only in the last half-century or so have portable power tools evolved from curiosities to job-site essentials. Sure, in countless centuries before that, houses were built, repaired and rebuilt by hand with simple tools that rewarded a craftsman's touch. But the new materials and crushing schedules typical of modern house building call for something more. As Norm will tell you, hand-sawing lengthwise down the length of a plywood sheet is no picnic, nor is it as accurate as zipping through sheets with a circular saw. He wouldn't think of ditching his power tools to relive the early days of completely hand-tooled houses, nor would Tom. They are, after all, practical men, New Yankees, and if they can do a better job or the same job faster by plugging something in, they will. *** Hand tools have a place, of course, and in the companion volume to this book you'll find out where it is. Here, though, you'll learn about power tools from Norm and Tom, as well as from other craftsmen. You'll find out about the features you need and the ones you don't, described by guys who know. You'll apprentice to master craftsmen to find out just what they look for in a particular tool and, most importantly, why. Unlike a hand tool, a power tool won't seduce you with exotic woods and gleaming steel, or invoke exquisite memories of fragrant shavings, and it won't give you thrills as an objet d'art parked on a living-room shelf. Nope. It's hard work and lots of it that warrants the speed and accuracy of a power tool; houses are made with nothing less.

—THE EDITORS

[**bandsaws**]

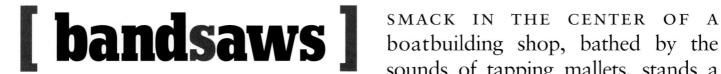

SMACK IN THE CENTER OF A boatbuilding shop, bathed by the sounds of tapping mallets, stands a cast-iron totem surrounded by partly completed dories and pea pods: a band saw. At the rumbling saw's wear-polished table, an apprentice stands in quiet reverie, gently coaxing mahogany through its moving blade. A nudge to the left, then to the right, and the board becomes a sweetly curved transom. If you're going to build boats, you'd better learn how to use a band saw. But other woodworkers, too, know that the saw offers a combination of speed, precision, safety, efficiency and quiet unmatched by any other cutting tool.

Compared with band saws, circular saws and tablesaws have ludicrously thick blades (that cut only in straight lines), paltry cutting depths, and they wail painfully while spraying sawdust all over the place. Scroll saws, jigsaws and reciprocating saws can cut curves, but they vibrate wickedly and cut slowly. It's no wonder that Norm Abram turns to a bandsaw when he needs a round tabletop or fresh boards from an old beam.

The original band saw, patented in 1808, had a pair of water-powered iron wheels mounted one above the other on a wooden frame. Today's band saws operate on the same principle: Two (or more) wheels pull a loop of thin, toothed steel through a narrow hole in a worktable. Band saws for workshops range from bench-top versions with 9-inch wheels to 1,600-pound floor models with 37-inch wheels and the ability to rip beams nearly 2-feet thick in half lengthwise. Band saws are classified by wheel diameter, the dimension that determines the width of board that can pass between the blade and the narrow throat supporting the top wheel. Norm's 14-inch saw, for instance, has a 13¾-inch-wide throat capacity. Some band saws turn blades over three wheels, but what they gain in throat capacity they lose in frame stiffness, making it hard to tension the blade properly.

WHEEL GUARDS: Conceals spinning wheels; contains debris if blade breaks.

BLADE GUIDE: Keeps blade from bending backward or sliding sideways during cuts.

BASE: Supports full-size saws; can be closed type (as here) or an open framework.

Carbon steel is the least- expensive blade. It's fine for cutting wood, but glued woods and plastic dull it quickly; it won't cut steel. Bimetal blades cut metal; they have tough high-speed-steel (HSS) teeth joined to spring steel backs. Carbide teeth brazed onto spring-steel stay sharp longer, but they're expensive and brittle, and not meant for cutting metal. Use many-toothed blades for thin stock and sparsely toothed blades for thick boards.

[**bandsaws**]

THREE-WHEEL BENCHTOP: An idler (the third wheel) is the trick that allows unusually wide cuts on such a compact machine. The wheels are $6\frac{1}{2}$ inches in diameter. Maximum cutting depth: $3\frac{1}{2}$ inches. Throat capacity: 10 inches. Maximum blade width: $\frac{1}{4}$ inch. Motor: $\frac{1}{2}$ hp.

PIVOT HEAD: Unlike band saws with tilting tables, this one has tilting wheels instead, an arrangement that makes bevel cuts easier. Maximum cutting depth: 6 inches. Throat capacity: $11\frac{1}{2}$ inches. Maximum blade width: $\frac{1}{2}$ inch. Motor: $1\frac{1}{8}$ hp.

TWO-WHEEL BENCH TOP: A rack-and-pinion blade guard allows precise, nonslip adjustment. Maximum cutting depth: $5\frac{1}{4}$ inches. Throat capacity: $7\frac{5}{8}$ inches. Maximum blade width: $\frac{3}{8}$ inch. Motor: $\frac{1}{5}$ hp.

PICK A BAND SAW TO SUIT THE WORK YOU DO: NO SINGLE SAW DOES EVERYTHING WELL. BENCH-TOP MODELS ARE SUITED TO SMALL (OR PORTABLE) SHOPS AND LIGHT-DUTY CUTTING OF THIN MATERIALS. A FULL-SIZE BAND SAW TAKES MORE SPACE BUT CUTS THROUGH THICKER AND WIDER STOCK; IT CAN RESAW TOO.

choosing a band saw

❮❮ The original band saw, patented in 1808, had a pair of water-powered iron wheels mounted one above the other on a wooden frame. ❯❯

A band saw's other crucial dimension is cutting thickness: how far the upper blade guide can be positioned above the table. Bench top tools can accommodate pieces from 3 to 5 inches thick; Norm's 14-inch saw has a capacity of more than 6 inches, while the big resaw machine (a heavy-duty band saw with a wide blade) in the New Yankee Workshop can handle stock nearly 12 inches thick.

An underpowered saw cuts slowly, strains the blade and motor, and burns the work. It takes at least a ½-hp motor to cut cleanly through 3 to 5 inches of most hardwoods. Norm's 14-incher has a ¾-hp motor, and the resaw machine generates nearly 3 hp.

The real key to a band saw's performance, however, is the blade. Off the machine, the thin flexible coils seem incapable of slicing much more than stale bread. But when mounted and tightened taut as a piano string, this strip of steel—half the thickness of a dime and moving at 2,000 to 5,000 feet per minute—can slice through most anything.

Width determines much of how a blade cuts. The narrower its profile, the tighter the curves it can cut without twisting. A ⅛-inch blade, for instance can follow a ⅜-inch radius while a ¾-inch blade can only manage about 5½ inches. Wider blades, from ¾ inches to 2 inches or more, cut fast and straight, resist twisting and rarely break. Most often used for resawing thick boards, they only fit saws with wide wheels, powerful motors and heavy, stiff frames built to withstand the high tension that keeps them on course. Those who want to cut curvy *and* straight should either master the trick of changing blades or settle on a width that cuts both ways fairly well—¼ inch is a good compromise. Norm simply has two saws: a curve cutter, which spins blades from ⅛- to ¾ inch wide, and the resaw machine with its carbide-tipped 3-inch-wide blade.

Band saw blades are usually tightened to 15,000 pounds per square inch (psi), although tensions up to 27,500 psi may be necessary for resawing. Woodworkers who distrust their saw's tension gauge compare the note of a plucked blade to a tuning fork or a harmonica's pitch. Blades at 15,000 psi make an E; those at resawing tension produce a G-sharp.

It's counterintuitive, but the fewer teeth, the faster a blade will cut. A big resaw blade might have two or three teeth per inch (tpi), while a blade for scrollwork can have 20. Most woodworkers use blades with 4 to 10 tpi.

Despite their versatility, band saws are not perfect cutting tools. They aren't portable and can't make plunge cuts. But the smoothness of the skinny blade shooting through stock—it's the most pleasingly hypnotic way to part wood.

[**beltsanders**]

HERE'S A PROBLEM FOR YOU: Tom Silva once built 12 hefty display tables for a Boston-area farmer's market. Every table had four legs; every leg was secured by three birch pegs, and every peg stuck out half an inch. How long did it take him to make all the pegs perfectly flush? Using a belt sander and an 80-grit belt, he turned the 72 inches of protruding pegs to dust in less than seven minutes. That's one ruthless tool. Belt sanders are the chain saws of sanding machines: loud, agressive and very effective. Like sharks, they must roam constantly. Paused in one place, even for a second, they chew down the hardest wood.

you can get
more life out of any sanding belt if you clean it occasionally. Hold a crepe rubber cleaning block against the spinning belt to remove residue; you'll notice a big difference.

These brutes are simple tools: a switch, a motor, a dust bag and two rollers to guide the sanding belt over a flat base plate. The motor drives only the rear roller; the front roller is a tensioned pulley that keeps the belt taut. Most belt sanders have a transversely mounted motor (perpendicular to and above the belt), but some compact models have in-line motors.

Belt size distinguishes one sander from another. The biggest use belts 4 inches wide and 24 inches in circumference, but there also are 4-by-21, 3-by-24, 3-by-21 and even diminutive 3-by-18 models, as well as a few specialty sanders with belts barely an inch wide. Tom prefers broad 4-by-24 brutes that can rip through decades of paint or level wide swaths of wood. These muscle machines are heavy—some tip the scales at 15 pounds—but that's not a problem for Tom. He can usually flop wood across a couple of sawhorses and let the sander's weight do the work as he steers.

Norm Abram prefers the maneuverability of a smaller sander. "When you're trying to

sand door casings without taking them off the jambs," he says, "a 3-by-21 is nice." Some weigh less than six pounds, light enough to use one-handed. And clamped to a workbench or upended on a special stand, any belt sander turns into a stationary tool that can trim a whisker off the back of a poor-fitting miter.

The only way to know which belt sander is best for you, says Tom, is to "heft a bunch of 'em." Lift one off a store's display shelf, attach the dust bag, then move the tool back and forth as if sanding the top of a coffee table. Tip it sideways and sand the table's edges, then round over some sharp corners and smooth a table leg or two. Note the feel of the handles as the tool's position changes, and see if the dust bag gets in the way. Install and remove a sanding belt (some belt-release levers are hard to reach and distressingly stiff). Repeat the routine with several other sanders.

Belt sanders generate lots of sawdust, a known health risk so Tom hooks his sander to a shop vac whenever he can, even for modest

AUXILIARY KNOB: A hand here helps the sander stay on the work. This one is removable.

DUST BAG: Collects sawdust and paint kicked up by sanding. Bags may be front-mounted (as here) or located beside, behind or above the sander.

MAIN HANDLE: A good grip here holds the sander in check. Small sanders such as this one can be operated with one hand.

TRIGGER SWITCH: Turns the sander on and off; a lock button keeps the sander going without requiring finger pressure on the switch. Switches may be linked to variable-speed controls.

FRONT ROLLER: Unlike the rear roller, the one in front freewheels. Its axis can be adjusted in order to center the belt.

REAR ROLLER: Also called the drive roller, it is linked to the sander's motor via drive belt or drive chain.

BASE PLATE: Also called a wear plate or shoe, this flat surface presses the sanding belt against the work. Replace if worn.

SANDING BELT: A loop of abrasive paper or cloth that comes in several widths, lengths and grits. Cloth belts are best.

BELT-RELEASE LEVER: The lever releases tension on the belt for belt removal.

[beltsanders]

sanding jobs. He finds vacuum-assisted belts clog less, so they're able to cut faster; they also throw even less sawdust into the air. Old paint may harbor lead, making vacuum pickup and a respirator essential. Before laying a sander on anything, though, Tom always checks to see how well the belt is tracking over the base plate. If a belt wanders, he slowly turns the tracking knob as the sander is running until the belt centers over the plate and stays there. It isn't necessary to do this often; Tom tracks his sander only when switching belts, and some sanders have automatic belt tracking anyway. Another change in belt sanders is the addition of variable-speed controls. But Tom prizes technique over technology and likes his belt sanders simple; no need, says he, for more than one speed. A slow speed, however, prevents the tool from cutting so quickly, a plus in the hands of an inexperienced user.

Most problems occur when sanders are pressed hard. As Norm notes, "It takes a fair amount of practice to use a belt sander because the portion of the belt on the plate is so small in relation to the rest of the tool." But once you know how to drive one, this bulldozer of a tool can be driven like a sports car.

* * *

SANDING BELTS

A SANDING BELT'S WORK IS DONE BY LEGIONS OF TINY, CHISEL-SHARP abrasive granules, or grit, graded by size from supercoarse 24 grit to silky 320. Closed-coat belts pack the grit tightly; they're best for sanding metal and hardwoods. Open-coat belts space out the grit to reduce clogging; they work better on soft, pitchy woods like pine and for stripping paint or varnish.

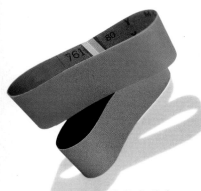

Choose belts by their backing and grit; color is mostly a branding device.

Aluminum-oxide grit is inexpensive and good for general-duty wood sanding. Alumina-zirconia belts (usually blue) or ceramic aluminum oxide belts (usually purple) stay sharp longer but are pricey and hard to find in grits finer than 120. Tom never uses belts finer than 150 grit anyway; that's territory he covers with a random-orbit sander.

Grit is embedded in resin atop a backing of paper or cloth. The best belts are cloth: tightly woven cotton, polyester or a blend of the two. Polyester is more durable than pure cotton, but you won't always know which is which: belt makers don't always label the backing.

All belts once had lumpy glue-and-lap joints that would self-destruct if spun in the wrong direction (arrows on the backing show which way they're supposed to go). Newer bidirectional belts can run in either direction. They last 10 to 15 percent longer and sand smoother than old-style belts. Tom cleans or replaces a belt when his sander turns tame; worn or clogged belts have lousy traction.

Belt Stripper: Intended for close-quarters work and sanding deck detail, this sander has a belt only 1⅛-inch wide. A removable handle allows the tool to sneak into unusually tight places.

Gritty Bitty: A slender nose, variable speed and a short 1-½-inch wide belt make this model aggressive but easy to control. The belt tracks over two platens.

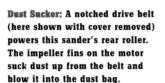

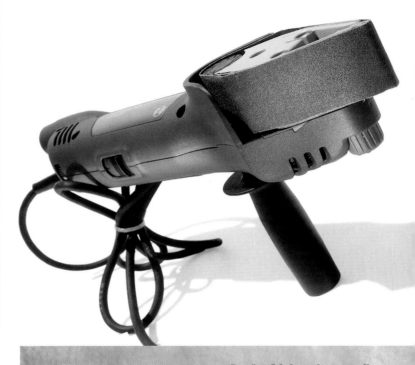

Dust Sucker: A notched drive belt (here shown with cover removed) powers this sander's rear roller. The impeller fins on the motor suck dust up from the belt and blow it into the dust bag.

Bag Get: A belt sander on a roll creates clouds of dust; collection bags make breathing easier. Most mount alongside the tool, but some mount at the top, swiveling clear of the work. Many sanders can be attached to a shop vac.

[bench**g**rinders]

THE LANDSCAPE OF A MACHINE SHOP IS AN alien world: Mountainous gray machines loom above a littered plain of razor-sharp slivers and gleaming curls of spent metal. At the periphery of this stygian scene, off in a quiet corner and caked with the grime of decades, is an island of mechanical simplicity: a bench grinder. Just a one-speed, fractional-horse motor bolted to a table, it's a squat metal toad of a tool with two gritty wheels sprouting like ears from either side, and it's ready to work miracles on metal.

SPARK ARRESTER: Bats down bits of hot metal before they circle the wheel and hit your hand.

EYE SHIELD: Protects the user against sparks and flying debris. It can be flipped out of the way when grinding large items.

WHEEL GUARD: Removable for wheel changing; confines debris.

After a 10-minute buff by a bench grinder, this prize from a Wall Street renovation glowed.

WORK LIGHT: An adjustable lamp highlights sharpened edges and makes accurate grinding easier and safer.

DRESSER: Dressing restores worn wheels to flatness; this tool stores a dresser.

MOTOR HOUSING: A grinder's induction motor is completely sealed.

8-in. Bench Grinder
1 Horsepower
8 x 1 x 5/8-in. Wheels
5/8-in. Arbor

SPECIFICATIONS
Heavy Duty Induction Motor
1 HP - 1.1 Amps 3450 RPM (No-Load Speed)
120-v., 60-Hz, AC only.

WARNING

FOR YOUR OWN SAFETY: Read and understand enclosed owner's manual before operating this grinder. ALWAYS wear eye protection which complies with current ANSI Standard Z87.1. ONLY USE GRINDING WHEELS SUITABLE FOR SPEED OF THIS GRINDER. Failure to heed all warnings could result in serious bodily injury.

GRINDING WHEEL: Aluminum-oxide wheels such as this one come standard on most grinders but aren't the best for fine work.

TOOL REST: A stout rest pivots to support grinding, but it should fit much closer to the wheel than this.

SPINDLE HOUSING (visible beneath eye shield): A single shaft powers both wheels; the housing protects it.

QUENCHING BASIN: Tools being ground won't overheat if dipped periodically in the basin's water.

[benchgrinders]

With a steady hum and a halting, hissing scrape, a grinder can sharpen a chisel or touch up a mower blade or, in a spray of sparks, revive an ax and scour rough welds smooth. Fitted with a wire wheel, it chews off decades of paint from old door hardware or claws through rust on a shovel. With a flannel-soft buffing wheel, it can polish silver to a mirror shine, restore the gloss to a '49 Harley or make pewter candlesticks glow like a winter sunrise, and it's unsurpassed for restoring architectural hardware. Russ Morash, *This Old House* executive producer, regularly grinds fresh edges on his garden spade with his ancient benchtop tool. "That's the secret to getting the most out of a spade," he confides. Tom Silva keeps a bench grinder in his truck and lugs it out to sharpen cold chisels, regrind worn screwdrivers, shorten bolts and sharpen drill bits. Norm Abram uses his to put a hollow-ground edge on woodworking chisels.

Some woodworkers, however, don't quite trust bench grinders, citing their tendency to damage fine tool steel. But that's like boring into concrete and blaming the drill for messing up a good spade bit. With the right wheel, the right speed and a touch of finesse, a grinder is

The side of the thick, 8-inch brown wheel, not the edge, offers more grinding surface and a wide selection of surface speeds, but it won't produce a hollow-ground edge. A basin-fed water-drip system keeps wheel and tools cool. The big wheel runs at 400 rpm, while its 5-inch-diameter cousin (mounted conventionally) clocks in at 3,600 rpm.

Sloshing through a water basin at 100 rpm keeps the 10-inch grinding wheel of this sharpening specialist cool and clean. Its dry leather companion wheel strops edges to razor sharpness. A host of accessories clamp to the tool support, permitting precise sharpening of everything from lathe tools to plane irons.

« Grind off too much too fast with the wrong wheel and you'll ruin the steel's temper by overheating it. »

capable of surprisingly fine work. Part of the grinder's bad-boy reputation stems from the gray aluminum-oxide wheels it's most often fitted with. The durable granules of these wheels are blocky and coarse, making them great for hogging off metal quickly but not so good for sharpening, even in the finest grits. "Grind off too much too fast with the wrong wheel," Tom warns, "and you'll ruin the steel's

temper by overheating it." When steel turns blue, the temper is gone, along with any ability to hold an edge. The damage must be ground away—carefully—to expose new metal. Dipping a tool in water is one way to keep it cool, and many bench grinders include a quenching basin for this purpose. Far better for edge tools are white aluminum-oxide wheels. They wear faster and cut slower, but their angular grains shear steel for a finer finish with less heat.

Unlike the universal motors found in portable power tools, bench-grinder motors are driven by induction, a propulsion method suited to gritty shop environments. Induction motors are sealed within their metal housings, have no brushes to wear out, no air vents to clog, few moving parts and can spin relentlessly at peak horsepower without overheating. If a grinder runs when first plugged in, it'll probably run forever. "Dad bought the one we have when he was in the business," says Tom, and the grinder Russ uses is likewise a geezer.

The downside of an induction motor is its single-minded inability to turn at more than one speed. There are high-speed grinders that spin their wheels at 3,450 rpm—perfect for grinding and buffing—and there are low-speed grinders that hum along at a sedate 1,725 rpms or so—good for sharpening. But to get two speeds, you'll have to buy two grinders or get a relatively expensive hybrid, geared-down system with whetted sharpening wheels. The

Gearing allows the same motor to turn a thick, 10-inch sharpening wheel through a water trough at 70 rpm while its companion, a 5-inch grinding wheel, spins at 3,450 rpm. The result: a tool that grinds with spark-and-speed enthusiasm or cool restraint.

[benchgrinders]

low-speed bench grinder, by the way, is virtually indistinguishable from its reckless cousin, except for its higher price (about double that of the high-speed version).

That's not the whole speed story, however. Because a wheel moves faster at its rim than at its center, bigger wheels have higher rim speeds. An 8-inch wheel on a high-speed grinder, for example, has a rim speed of 6,900 feet per minute, a third faster than a 6-inch wheel.

Bench grinders often share another common failing: flimsy tool rests. The rests on many grinders flex and wiggle and have limited ability to adjust to the ever-shrinking wheel; they're an inconvenience as well as a safety hazard. Add-on tool rests that bolt to a workbench offer more adjustability. Then no matter how small a wheel gets, the rest's edge can always be within ⅛ inch of the wheel.

Properly equipped, the unassuming bench grinder is the sorcerer of the shop, giving new life to old metal. When touched by its wheels, a dull blade cuts, a rusty hinge swings, a tarnished doorknob gleams. In its warm, reassuring thrum, there is the hint of rebirth.

It's The Abrasive rubbed into felt that does the polishing, not the wheel itself. For convenience, buffing abrasives are usually embedded in pastel-like sticks (right) that are briefly held against a spinning wheel. **1. Jeweler's rouge** is very fine and brings out the luster of gold and silver. **2. Tripoli** is a general-purpose abrasive that removes minor imperfections and shines brass, aluminum and pewter. **3. Emery** is aggressive for coarse buffing and rust removal. **4. Plastic compound** buffs out scratched acrylic. **5. White rouge** brightens stainless, chrome and nickel. **6. Stainless** is similar to white rouge.

TECHNIQUES

Sharpening: When grinding an edge (above), use the grinder's tool rest for support. Sharpening is easier to control and more efficient when the wheel's top spins toward the tool's edge. Here a gloved hand pins a hatchet to the rest. As the other hand steers, metal pivots in a sweeping arc over the wheel. This grinder's spark arrester should be closer to the wheel; a ⅛-inch clearance is best.

Buffing: A spinning flannel wheel dosed with buffing compound can get metal so hot (and in a surprisingly short time) that the surface momentarily liquefies. Wear gloves, keep the metal moving, and always keep the work lower than the spindle, or else the wheel will yank whatever you're buffing out of your hands. For best results, use separate wheels for each buffing compound—the disks are easily mounted and removed—so that you don't scratch with a contaminated wheel what you meant to polish.

choosing a wheel

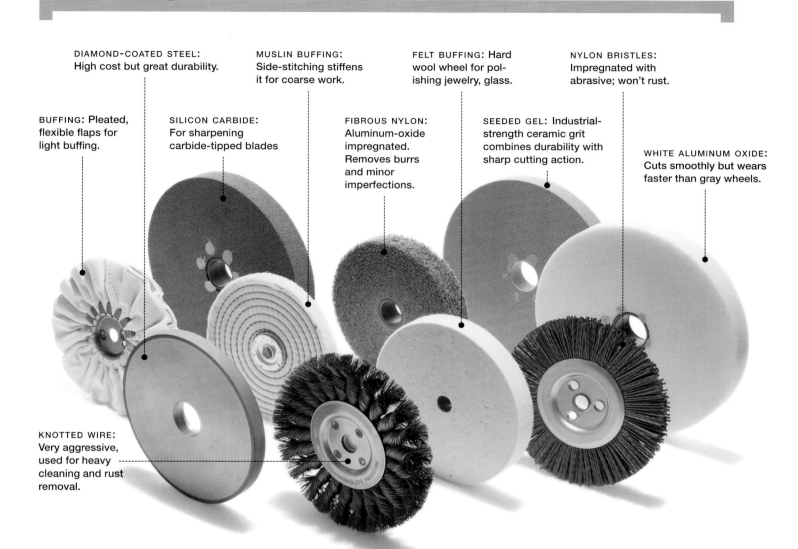

DIAMOND-COATED STEEL: High cost but great durability.

MUSLIN BUFFING: Side-stitching stiffens it for coarse work.

FELT BUFFING: Hard wool wheel for polishing jewelry, glass.

NYLON BRISTLES: Impregnated with abrasive; won't rust.

BUFFING: Pleated, flexible flaps for light buffing.

SILICON CARBIDE: For sharpening carbide-tipped blades

FIBROUS NYLON: Aluminum-oxide impregnated. Removes burrs and minor imperfections.

SEEDED GEL: Industrial-strength ceramic grit combines durability with sharp cutting action.

WHITE ALUMINUM OXIDE: Cuts smoothly but wears faster than gray wheels.

KNOTTED WIRE: Very aggressive, used for heavy cleaning and rust removal.

GETTING THE BEST FROM A BENCH GRINDER IS A MATTER OF MATCHING A WHEEL TO THE WORK AND THE GRINDER TO THE WHEEL. MAKE SURE THE WHEEL'S HOLES MATCH THE GRINDER'S SPINDLE, WHICH COMES IN 1/2-, 5/8- AND 3/4-INCH ARBOR DIAMETERS. SECOND, CHECK THE WHEEL'S SPEED LIMIT; TOO MANY RPMS CAN TEAR IT APART. THIRD, BEFORE MOUNTING ANY GRINDING WHEEL, NEW OR OLD, TEST IT FOR CRACKS. HOLD THE WHEEL ON A FINGER AND TAP IT WITH THE HANDLE OF A SCREWDRIVER. GOOD WHEELS RING; BAD WHEELS THUD AND MIGHT EXPLODE WHILE TURNING. IN THE BATTLE BETWEEN GRIT AND STEEL, A NEW WHEEL'S CRISP, FLAT RIM GRADUALLY GETS DISHED AND BECOMES GLAZED—CLOGGED WITH METAL AND SPENT ABRASIVE. DRESSING RESTORES RIM FLATNESS.

[**biscuitjoiners**]

A BISCUIT JOINER AT rest is inscrutable. No blade bespeaks action, no gritty belt or bristly wheel implies purpose—the squat hobbit just sits there. That is, until Tom Silva grabs it. *Zeerip! Zeerip!* goes the tool as Tom plunges it repeatedly into a doorjamb, stitching semicircular slots into the edge. After cutting matching slots in a piece of trim, Tom butters all the cuts with yellow carpenter's glue, reaches into his tool belt and pulls out a handful of 3-inch beechwood slivers that look like a tiny flattened footballs. He slips a "biscuit" into each of the jamb's slots and slaps the trim over them. Voilà— in about the same time that it takes to make a weak joint with glue alone, Tom has made a strong one using biscuits and the odd-bodkin biscuit joiner.

The first biscuiting tools in the United States were imported from Europe by the Lamello Company in the early 1980s. Not much more than an angle grinder with a 4-inch diameter (or smaller) saw blade and a chunky L-shaped fence on the nose, the biscuit joiner is finally beginning to break out of the woodworkers' insular domain and into the world of the homeowner. It may be, in fact, the perfect power tool: durable, forgiving and so easy to use that a novice can improve his wood-working abilities immediately. Professionals know a good idea when they see it. When Tom first picked one up 10 years ago, it was love at first plunge: "I saw instantly that it made wood joints strong and easier to assemble."

Before biscuits, a strong joint took lots of time both in the learning and the making. Dovetail and mortise-and-tenon joints need precision sawing and chiseling to create mating surfaces that meet exactly. Spline joints require a router or table saw, a sure hand and custom-sawn splines. Dowel joints use standard drill

A biscuit joiner's carbide-tipped blade plunge-cuts a half-oval slot into all manner of synthetic materials, including solid-surface countertops and Lucite (above), but the tool is most often used to create joints that hold pieces of wood together.

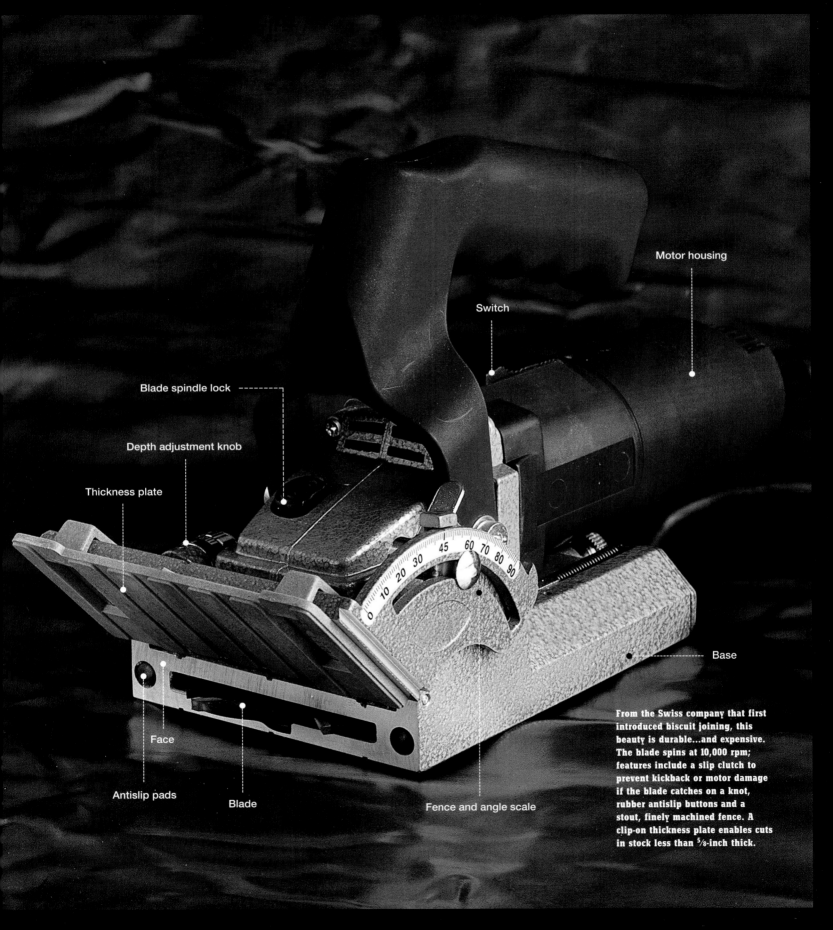

Motor housing

Switch

Blade spindle lock

Depth adjustment knob

Thickness plate

0 10 20 30 45 60 70 80 90

Base

Face

Antislip pads

Blade

Fence and angle scale

From the Swiss company that first introduced biscuit joining, this beauty is durable...and expensive. The blade spins at 10,000 rpm; features include a slip clutch to prevent kickback or motor damage if the blade catches on a knot, rubber antislip buttons and a stout, finely machined fence. A clip-on thickness plate enables cuts in stock less than ⁵⁄₈-inch thick.

[biscuitjoiners]

bits and wood pegs but demand absolute precision in layout and drilling; if one dowel is just a smidgen off, it will ruin the joint. Contractors and homeowners have had little time for such nonsense. When installing trim work, they've used glue, nails and a prayer, and hardly seem surprised when the joints open up later. Biscuits can't match the strength of tenons, splines or dowels, but in undemanding joints, they're stronger than glue alone. "I had to pull out a fresh-glued biscuit joint once," Tom recalls. "It wasn't fun."

Despite the unfamiliarity of a typical biscuit joiner, the tool is easy to operate: Just hold the spring-loaded fence against a hard

surface, turn the motor on and push. The carbide-tipped circular blade slides forward only enough to make its kerf, usually ½-inch deep. As the tool is pulled off the work, the fence covers the blade, protecting both it and the operator from harm.

This is a forgiving system. "You don't have to measure a layout," says Tom. He simply pencils a line across the joint and uses his line as a target for the tool's index marks. Joints invariably fit because mating pieces can slide lengthwise about ⅛ inch without binding on the biscuit. And there's no fighting with glue-slick wood; biscuits hold mating surfaces in perfect alignment as the glue dries. "It's like having three hands," says Tom.

A biscuit joiner has few quirks. There's a tendency for the blade to pull to the left as it grabs the wood, but a thumb on the fence, and the slip-resisting prongs, pads or buttons on the tool's face minimize or eliminate sideways movement. Tom also makes sure the face rests flat against the work. "It's more important to keep that correct than worry about small differences in blade position," he says.

The applications seem endless. "There's always a use for a biscuit," Tom says. He rattles off the ways he uses them now: assembling exterior corner boards, indexing the long miters on soffits, attaching cabinet stiles to rails, joining boards edge to edge to make a tabletop, installing deck railings, even assembling two-by-fours into an inexpensive bunk bed for his kids. Tom says his biscuit joiner has become as essential as his ever-present cell phone. "I could work without it," he says, "but I wouldn't want to."

Biscuit On Board: After cutting all the slots, Tom spreads carpenter's glue (below) on the mating surfaces and into each slot. A small, disposable glue brush helps, but Tom often uses a tool that's more readily available: his finger. After pushing biscuits firmly into each slot on one board, Tom assembles and clamps the joint. Moisture will swell each biscuit, making a tight mechanical bond that complements the glue's bond. This works only with glues that are moisture-curing, however, not with polyurethane glues.

TECHNIQUES

Cutting A Slot: Tom sets the depth dial to suit the biscuit's size, flips down the fence and adjusts the blade's height to about half the board's thickness. The whole process takes less than 10 seconds. To cut the slot, he lines up the fence's red index mark with his pencil line, turns the tool on and pushes it into the wood. A thumb on the fence steadies the tool and keeps it from rocking.

Fitted with either a 2-inch or a 4-inch blade, this joiner can biscuit big and small. It has a rear-mounted switch, seven depth settings and a gritty, full-length antislip pad. (10,000 rpm)

A low profile puts the user's hand in line with the easy-to-change 4-inch blade. The fence has rack-and-pinion gearing, six depth settings and a full-length rubber antislip pad. (10,000 rpm)

This upright, D-handled biscuit joiner has a trigger switch, a 4-inch blade, three depth settings and retracting antislip pins that minimize or eliminate the need to penetrate the wood. (8,000 rpm)

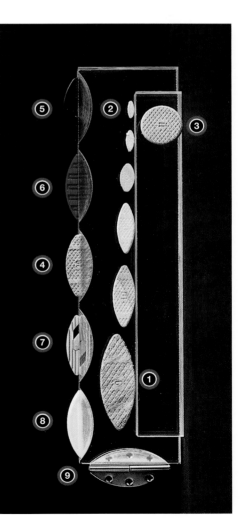

The 2-inch blade on this model cuts slots for the tiny biscuits used in picture frames. Features include a reversible 45- and 90 degree fence, a rubber antislip pad and 3 depth settings. (20,000 rpm)

A rechargeable 12-volt battery makes this cordless joiner portable, a plus when trimming out doors and windows. It has a 4-inch blade, six depth settings and two rubber antislip buttons. (24,000 rpm)

A Batch Of Biscuits: The best wood biscuits are beech; it takes glue well and swells predictably. Die-cut from solid wood and imprinted with a pattern that improves moisture absorption, they range widely in size. 1. A 3½ inch long S-6 biscuit is for thick stock. 2. The diminutive ¾-inch R-2 is for picture frames. 3. Round biscuits fit in kerfs cut by a router's slot-cutting bit. 4. Tom's favorite wood biscuit, the No. 20, suits many joining jobs. 5. UV-resistant polypropylene biscuits space wooden deck boards uniformly and anchor them invisibly. 6. Plastic clamping biscuits grab wood without glue; they're used with wood biscuits in hard-to-clamp joints. 7. Interlocking aluminum plates allow joint disassembly. 8. Plastic biscuits join slabs of solid-surface countertop. 9. This hinge isn't a biscuit, but fits into a biscuit slot.

[**chainsaws**]

NASTY, BRUTISH AND SHORT: that's the ideal homeowner's chain saw. A smallish saw with no more than a 16-inch bar can transform the tangled mess of a fallen tree into tidy piles of kindling and firewood. Cycling between a sputter and a wail, its single-cylinder engine always lets you know it's in the neighborhood. The chain saw's image is tarnished somewhat by movie massacres and gruesome logger lore. An unguarded row of razor-sharp teeth can, after all, do a lot of damage moving at 50 feet per second. Yet if used properly, no tool can match its furious efficiency. This Old House landscaping contractor Roger Cook has logged countless hours with chain saws mighty and modest. "It's absolutely essential to respect what the saw can do to you," he warns. He makes limbing a downed tree and bucking it into rounds look no riskier than lopping off a Thanksgiving drumstick. But his technique, like that of a careful chess master playing against a capable and unpredictable foe, blends caution with strategy.

You won't find them often on job sites, but chain saws do have a place there. A log home's painstaking joinery, for example, is possible only by means of phenomenal skill and a chain saw. Remodelers have less ambitious uses for the tool, which can quickly cut a beam or a post to length or cut out rotten joists flush with the subfloor. Production framers have been known to chain-saw bundles of studs to length—in their world, time is more precious than precision. When it comes to moving houses, a chain saw will size support timbers or slice a house in half.

In the woods, proper cutting technique is crucial, and the right gear will increase your chances of leaving the woods in one piece. Roger wears a hard hat with a flip-down face shield and integral earmuffs. Chain-saw chaps protect his legs, and leather boots with a chain-choking inner lining shield his feet.

Starting A Saw: Starting a saw is easiest on the ground. Clear debris from a small area to avoid being skewered by sticks thrown backward by the chain. Pin down the rear handle with your boot, grasp the front handle firmly, then pull the starter handle. Several pulls are often needed to coax older engines. When the saw roars to life, get both hands on it before moving your boot. **Trimming Limbs:** Work from tip to stump along a tree, taking weight off to minimize shifting. Roger cuts limbs flush with the log—stubs left behind make rounds tougher to split. Most hand injuries come from trying to hold the saw with one hand while steadying a limb with the other. Instead, support a limb so you can keep both hands on the saw. **Notch-Cutting Limbs:** Long limbs may pinch the blade as they drop, so Roger notches the underside of a big limb first, then finishes it off with a cut from the top. Be alert to signs of pinching: The saw will labor, then seem to freeze in the cut. Stop the saw and use a plastic wedge, not metal, to pry open the cut just enough to free the bar. **Bucking Logs:** Make several cuts about two-thirds of the way through a log that's fully on the ground. This prevents pinching and keeps chains out of the dirt. Use the saw's gripper spikes (beneath the blade) to pivot the saw through the log. Let the saw idle before pulling it from a cut; then turn the log and finish the cut.

Starting A Saw

Trimming Small Limbs

Notch-Cutting Big Limbs

Bucking Downed Logs

[chainsaws]

CHAIN: Adjust tension frequently and wear gloves when handling. Anti-kick-back chains are the safest.

BAR: A length of 14 to 16 inches is best for most homeowners.

BLADE BRAKE: Saw kickback drives hand into blade brake and instantly stops chain. Use it like a parking brake to lock the chain when you carry the saw. Always engage the brake when not cutting. Not found on all saws.

DANGER ZONE: If teeth in this area contact wood, the whole saw will kick back violently.

OPTIMAL CUTTING ZONE: Safest place to cut.

WHEN USING A CHAIN SAW, as he has for more than 20 years without an accident, Roger follows these guidelines: **1.** Never cut with a dull chain. Before firing up a saw, check for worn, chipped or gouged teeth. Roger touches up his chains with a round file, but unless you know how, it's best to keep several sharp chains on hand and take dull ones to a professional for sharpening. One chain can last through about 20 sharpenings before it's junk. **2.** Before firing up your saw, walk around the entire tree to see what's supporting it. If the bulk of the log is off the ground, get it on terra firma promptly. If it's hung up on vines or other trees, pull it down with ropes. If it's caught on a power line, call the power company or a tree service–this is no job for amateurs. **3.** Check the terrain. Could the tree twist or roll if you cut off a limb? Plan an escape route. **4.** Study the limbs. Bent ones can pop like springs; relieve pressure by carefully backcutting small limbs (two inches or less in diameter) or by notch-cutting larger ones. **5.** When cutting, keep the elbow of your non-trigger hand locked straight; if the saw kicks, you will have more control. Hold the saw close to your body, spread your feet slightly and nestle the engine against the tree. For small limbs, try to stand so the tree is between you and the chain. **6.** If you can, run the fuel tank dry when you're finished. Then clean the air filter and use an old paintbrush to clear sawdust and dirt from the bar and engine fins. Next session, fuel up with the right gas-oil mix and top off the chain-oil reservoir.

FRONT HANDLE: Always keep hand on top of handle, behind blade brake, with thumb locked underneath.

PULL ROPE: Starts engine. Keep spare on hand in case it breaks.

AIR FILTER: Brush off debris after each use. Clean with solvent recommended by manufacturer.

TRIGGER LOCK: Press to free trigger. Releasing this lock idles engine.

CHOKE: Open to start engine. Closes automatically.

TRIGGER: Engages chain and controls engine speed.

CHAIN-OIL RESERVOIR: Lubricates chain and bar to prevent over-heating. Most saws have automatic oilers.

STARTER: Keep the protective engine fins free of debris.

FUEL TANK: Use recommended mix of unleaded gas and two-cycle oil.

[circular**saws**]

It was the workhorse. We did everything

with the circular saw, or so it seems.

NORM ABRAM FIRST GOT HIS HANDS ON A CIRCULAR SAW AT 14, HELPING his carpenter father on various job sites. These days Norm needn't ask so much of his circular saw, so he uses it mostly for its ideal purpose—cutting through plywood and framing lumber with straight-arrow accuracy and furious dispatch. Unlike many power tools these days, the circular saw remains steadfastly single-speed, and many who pick it up for the first time figure that it couldn't be that tough to use: Just pull the trigger and let 'er rip.

HEIGHT ADJUSTMENT LEVER: Lifts or lowers blade to control depth of cut.

MAIN HANDLE: Contains trigger switch.

DUST PORT: This saw can be fitted with a dust bag.

MOTOR: On left side of blade. Removable caps make brush replacement easy.

BEVEL ADJUSTMENT: Tilts saw to one side for making bevel cuts up to 45 degrees.

GUARD LEVER: Used to slide guard away from blade while starting cuts on thin stock or when making plunge cuts.

BLADE GUARD: Prevents accidental contact with blade.

SAW BASE: Should be stiff without being heavy.

PROUDLY MADE IN USA

[circularsaws]

Indeed, it takes a few seconds, nothing more, to slice through a 2x4. Do it wrong, though, and you'll remember those seconds forever. Norm's circular-saw cutting techniques may seem overly cautious, but more than 30 years of accident-free work with the saw is a great endorsement.

Setting the proper blade depth is crucial, he advises, to minimize kickback and expose fewer clawing teeth beneath the cut. To lop off the end of a 2x4, for example, Norm unplugs the saw and adjusts the saw to a depth that leaves the lowest tooth no more than about $\frac{1}{8}$ inch beneath the wood. After marking a cut line, he guides the saw along the edge of a square. Why guide a simple crosscut? "If you turn the saw even slightly after it's partway through the cut," warns Norm, "the blade binds up and the saw can kick back at you." A bonus: The square ensures a square cut.

Whatever your method, never lift the saw when the blade is still moving. Instead, push it completely through the wood in a single, fluid motion until the offcut drops free. Generally, Norm keeps the broadest part of the base on the "keep" part of the wood. Another tip: If you rock the saw forward and backward slightly as you get ready to cut, you can feel the front of the saw's base slap against the wood. That's when you know the saw is fully supported by the wood.

Plywood can be more difficult to crosscut than dimensional lumber. The pieces are big, the cuts are long, and the wood is more likely to splinter. Kickback is a particular risk because a sheet of plywood flexes readily, allowing the cut edges to pinch the blade. Proper support is essential. Norm lays several 2x4 supports over his sawhorses, adding more if the plywood is less than $\frac{1}{2}$-inch thick. To minimize splintering, he cuts with the

TOM SILVA LOVES HIS WORM-DRIVE CIRCULAR SAW BECAUSE IT CAN CHEW ALL DAY THROUGH THE TOUGHEST MATERIALS. THE WORM DRIVE GETS IT'S NAME FROM A PAIR OF MESHING GEARS —THE WORM AND THE WORM GEAR—THAT ORIENT THE MOTOR SHAFT AND THE BLADE ARBOR AT RIGHT ANGLES TO EACH OTHER (GIVING THE SAW IT'S CHARACTERISTIC SHAPE). A CRANKCASE-LIKE RESERVOIR FILLED WITH OIL KEEPS THE TWO GEARS LUBRICATED AND LETS THE SAW RUN SOMEWHAT MORE QUIETLY THAN A SIDEWINDER. BUT POWER COMES AT A PRICE: THE TOOL IS CONSIDERABLY HEAVIER THAN ITS COUSIN.
WORM-DRIVE SAWS LOVE BIG WORKLOADS, SUCH AS PRODUCTION HOUSE FRAMING OR SLICING STONE. A PARTICULAR ADVANTAGE OF A WORM-DRIVE: THE BLADE IS ON THE LEFT OF THE MOTOR, A LOCATION THAT OFFERS THE BEST VIEW OF THE CUT LINE.

worm-drive saws

Starting The Cut: The leading edge of a saw's blade guard can "hang up" on the edge of a plywood sheet at the beginning of a cut, preventing the saw from moving forward. To avoid this (below), Norm pivots the guard just enough to clear the surface of the plywood before he starts the saw and moves it forward. Once the saw's base passes the edge of the plywood, he releases the guard. Even with one finger on guard duty, though, Norm keeps both hands on the saw handles to resist any kickback.

Cutting Plywood: Plywood (above) is more flexible than lumber, and cutting it calls for particular care to prevent kickback. After supporting the sheet on sawhorses, Norm adjusts the saw's blade to barely cut through the material. With less blade in the cut, there's less blade for the plywood to pinch should it flex unexpectedly.

Sighting The Cut: Norm's saw is a sidewinder—the blade is on a shaft that's linked to the motor alongside. Unlike a worm-drive circular saw, a sidewinder has its motor on the left-hand side of the blade. That means Norm has to lean over the saw to see precisely where the blade is cutting. When he's trying to follow a layout line very carefully, as above, Norm steers the saw with his right hand and guides the base with his left, his thumb parked securely on a small indentation in the corner of the saw's base. If he has to change position to complete a cut, he shuts off the saw before making a move.

plywood's good face down because a circular saw cuts cleanest where the teeth are entering the wood. After adjusting the blade depth, Norm sets up a self-clamping straightedge to guide the saw. As he cuts, the saw blade will barely graze the top of each 2x4. He never lifts the saw or pulls it backward while the blade is moving—that's asking for kickback. If the blade binds or the cut goes awry, Norm stops the saw before repositioning it.

To keep the saw from binding in the first place, particularly at the beginning of a cut, Norm delegates a finger to push on the blade guard lever, thus rotating the guard out of the way just enough to clear the wood. After the saw is fully engaged in the cut, he releases the lever and lets the spring-loaded guard snap back and ride against the wood.

The power and portability of a circular saw are both an asset and a liability. If its blade gets trapped in a cut, the whole saw will kick back violently—at the user. Take Norm's advice and always stand to the side of the saw, just in case. Check frequently to make sure small pieces of wood haven't wedged open the blade guard. If your saw doesn't sound right, shut it off and find the problem. It could be a dull or dirty blade.

[circularsaws]

To keep your saw fit, brush off the dust now and then so that the bevel adjustment and blade-depth levers are clear. If your saw binds or your cuts aren't square, sight down the base to see if it's square and parallel to the blade. Check all knobs and screws regularly to make sure they're tight, and check the electrical cord for wear (especially at either end) and damage.

With the right blade, a circular saw can chew through most anything. Unfortunately, however, a saw's power cord can enter the food chain quite by accident. "Everyone," says Norm, "will eventually cut off their own cord." Don't repair it, he says; it's easier and more prudent just replace the whole thing. If he has the choice of two replacement-cord lengths, Norm usually opts for the longer one. "For me," he says, " the longer the cord, the better, because I don't want the plug hanging up on the edge of the wood."

The only motor maintenance most people are likely to encounter is minor. If a saw sputters or sparks, brushes may be the problem. These small blocks of hardened carbon wear out after a while. The access caps on Norm's saw make brush changes easy. He simply unscrews each of the caps (carefully, because the brushes are spring-loaded), lifts the old brushes out and slips in a new set.

« **If its blade** gets trapped in a cut, the whole saw will kick back violently—at the user. Always stand to the side of the saw, just in case. »

choosing a blade

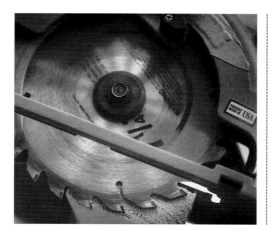

NO SAW AMOUNTS TO MUCH WITHOUT A GOOD BLADE. CIRCULAR-SAW BLADES ARE USUALLY 7 1/4 INCHES IN DIAMETER. A DECENT GENERAL-PURPOSE CARBIDE MODEL COSTS ABOUT $10 AND WILL STAY SHARP MUCH LONGER THAN A STEEL BLADE. NORM LIKES THIN-KERF BLADES BECAUSE THEY CUT FASTER WITH NOTICEABLY LESS EFFORT. NEW CARBIDE TEETH SHOULD BE SMOOTH AND SHINY, NOT CHIPPED OR PITTED; CHECK THEM WITH A LOW-POWER MAGNIFER. TO PROTECT BRITTLE CARBIDE, STORE EACH BLADE IN AN OLD MAILING ENVELOPE OR POCKET FOLDER. A DIRTY BLADE ISN'T SAFE TO CUT WITH. USE OVEN CLEANER TO DISSOLVE GUM AND PITCH WHEN THE BLADE IS OFF THE SAW.
AND NO MATTER WHAT THE BLADE, SET IT TO REDUCE KICKBACK: ITS TEETH SHOULD BARELY EXIT THE UNDERSIDE OF THE STOCK.

MASONRY BLADE: A toothless blade, this one is made from an abrasive material that grinds rather than cuts, making it ideal for scoring pavers or cutting bricks and concrete blocks. Beware of dust clouds.

PLYWOOD BLADE: Unlike construction blades that gobble wood, the steel teeth of this blade nibble it. The blade won't splinter thin surface veneers, so it's ideal for cutting cabinet-grade plywood and plywood paneling.

CHISEL-TOOTH STEEL BLADE: This blade probably came with your saw. It cuts fast (when sharp) and does a decent rip cut and crosscut. Few pros, however, would swap their carbide blades for easily dulled steel.

40-TOOTH TRIM BLADE: Premium carbide-tipped blades with 40 to 60 teeth are finish blades; they cut more slowly—but more smoothly—than similar blades with fewer teeth.

DECKING BLADE: Thin carbide teeth with raised shoulders cut smoothly through pressure-treated lumber and other decking woods. Radial slots in the blade reduce warping.

GENERAL-PURPOSE BLADE: Some blades cut faster, some smoother, but this 20-tooth carbide blade combines speed and long life with a fairly smooth cut. It must be resharpened at a saw shop, but a carbide blade is worth such effort. It's one of Norm's favorites.

REMODELING BLADE: Also called a demolition blade. Squared shoulders boost the shock resistance of the few (12 to 14) teeth on this carbide blade; use it on nail-embedded wood.

[cordless drills]

WHEN IT COMES TO DRILLING HOLES OR driving screws into nearly any surface, you just can't beat a cordless tool for convenience. "I don't even use a corded model anymore," says Tom Silva. "Unless I've got a pile of drywall to hang or a whole subfloor to screw off, it's faster to grab a cordless and go." He's not alone. "Plumbers, electricians, the guys who do the ductwork—they've all gone cordless," Tom adds.

Carpenters don't lug extension cords up and down ladders, heating contractors don't fillet their power cords on the edges of metal ducts, and nobody has to worry as much about the shock hazards of working where it's wet.

A cordless drill is hugely handy, but beefed-up models, called drill/drivers, are even more so, and that's why most powertool manufacturers emphasize them. A drill/driver is essentially a drill with added features (including a multisetting clutch) to handle the heavier stresses of screwdriving. That makes it more versatile than an ordinary drill. The

Variable-speed trigger

②

Paddle switch
with locking lever

Battery pack

①

Keyless chuck

High/Low speed
range switch

Clutch adjustment ring

③

④

Forward/
Reverse switch

⑤

Forward/Reverse switch

HIGH CAPACITY
9.6V

A Gallery Of Drills And Drivers: Like their corded cousins, cordless drills and drill/drivers suit various jobs. 1. A right-angle drill reaches into cabinet corners and drills between joists. 2. This powerful 12-volt drill/driver features a trigger-mounted variable-speed control and a fully enclosed handle that conceals storage for two bits. 3. The chuck of this drill is angled at 55 degrees to improve it's maneuverability in tight spaces. Two switches—a paddle and a trigger—enable various hand positions. 4. Tom prefers pistol-grip drill/drivers: He can put his muscle directly in line with the bit by centering his hand high on the tool, pulling the trigger with his lower two fingers. An auxiliary handle improves control. 5. Some users prefer the comfort of a T-handle drill/driver, though Tom says a T-handle's balance takes a while to get accustomed to.

batteries and battery chargers of both tools, however, are a lot better than they once were. Norm Abram's first cordless drill took about three hours to charge and wasn't much better than a Yankee screwdriver for driving screws. These days a drill/driver is ready to go in as little as 15 minutes, more than adequate to keep most people working steadily. Tom, however, packs two batteries to fit whatever tool he plans to use that day. One stays in the charger until the other weakens, and he swaps them back and forth all day to minimize downtime. As befits a busy contractor, he owns lots of cordless drill/drivers (but no cordless drills); some have 14.4-volt batteries. Unless you're using the tool professionally, though, a 9.6-volt drill/driver will be able to do most anything around your old house.

[cordlessdrills]

Most cordless drills have a variable-speed trigger switch: Slow speeds are for starting holes; fast speeds finish them. Drill/drivers have the same feature but with two separate ranges: a high-speed range for drilling holes and a high-torque range for driving screws (torque is a twisting force). When you shift into screwdriving range, an adjustable clutch inside the tool allows you to set screws at a consistent depth. Most drill/drivers have an electric brake too. When the trigger is completely released, the chuck stops instantly to keep you from overdriving a screw. Whatever its features, a drill or drill/driver should be comfortable to use—but that, Tom points out, is a personal thing. Be sure to heft a tool before you buy it, because they vary considerably in weight and balance.

The chuck of a drill or a drill/driver is rated according to the diameter of the largest bit shank it can hold: $\frac{1}{4}$ inch, $\frac{3}{8}$ inch, or $\frac{1}{2}$ inch are the sizes you'll encounter. The $\frac{3}{8}$-inch chuck is standard issue on general-duty tools (Tom wouldn't bother to use a smaller one anyway), and $\frac{1}{2}$ inch is essential for drills used to cut big holes or mix batches of plaster or stir 5-gallon buckets of paint. The biggest chuck decision, however, is whether or not to go keyless. A simple key with beveled teeth tightens most drill chucks; it works fine and tightens firmly—if you can find it. "A chuck key is the first thing you lose on a job," says Tom, even if it's clipped to the drill itself. There's nothing to lose with a keyless chuck: a pair of knurled rings lets you tighten or loosen the chuck by hand. "Keyed chucks? I won't miss 'em a bit," Tom says.

handy accessories

A CORDLESS DRILL WILL TAKE THE SAME ACCESSORIES AS A CORDED DRILL, INCLUDING GRINDING WHEELS, MIXING PADDLES, COUNTERSINKS AND ALL MANNER OF DRILL BITS. MOST OFTEN, THOUGH, IT WILL BE FITTED WITH SOMETHING TO DRIVE SCREWS. MOST CARPENTERS KEEP A FEW SCREWDRIVING BITS IN A POUCH OF THEIR TOOL BELT. THE HEX-SHANK BITS COME IN VARIOUS LENGTHS AND CAN FIT INTO A GUIDE SLEEVE OR INTO A QUICK-CHANGE CHUCK. BUT BE CAREFUL WHEN USING SLOTTED-SCREW BITS: THEY CAN EASILY MANGLE A SCREW HEAD.

A quick-change chuck is handy for switching quickly between drill bits and screwdriving bits. Hex shanks with grooved bases simply snap into place; a locking collar holds them securely.

Screwdriving bits

A screw-guide sleeve holds a bit magnetically while the sliding sleeve holds screws up to No. 10 diameter. The sleeve keeps screws from tipping or wandering as the drill spins.

Made in U.S.A.

A BATTERY CHARGER GENERATES HEAT, AND CONCENTRATING THAT heat into the short cycle typical of quick chargers can damage a battery (rechargeables are expensive to replace). "Smart" chargers get around this by using electronic circuitry to monitor the charging process and minimize heat buildup. Some even refuse to charge a sun-warmed battery until it has cooled. Other than keeping sawdust out, chargers need little care. "I've replaced a few," says Tom, "but that's mostly after something fell on them."

The battery of any cordless tool is actually a collection of batteries, called cells, wired together and fitted into a battery "pack." Each cell is rated at 1.2 volts; join 10 and you have a 12-volt pack. The greater the voltage, the more work the battery can do before it has to be recharged (and the heavier the tool). Battery packs usually last through 800 to 1,000 charging cycles; replacement packs generally cost $50 to $80. Some battery tips:

Unlike older nickel-cadmium batteries, the new nicads can be partially discharged and then recharged without any ill effect. But you'll get more life out of one if you recharge it only when the tool starts to feel sluggish. Don't wait until it stops dead—you can damage the cells if you discharge a battery too deeply.

It's against the law in some states to throw battery packs in the trash; heavy metals within the battery can leach into groundwater and pose a health hazard. Contact the drill manufacturer for recycling instructions.

Some batteries include a handy built-in LED readout that tells you how much charge is left at any given moment.

A battery charger and two batteries can usually keep up with most work. Indicator lights on the charger let you know how it's working. Store the charger and any extra batteries in a carrying case to prevent sawdust and dirt contamination. Batteries aren't interchangeable between manufacturers, however, and may not fit other cordless tools from the same manufacturer.

[detailsanders]

BEHOLD THE HUMAN hand, a splendid 27-bone marionette strung with tendon and muscle. It can boogie or waltz, crush or caress, speak for the mute and see for the blind. Alas, no other biomechanism is so supremely suited to the singular tedium of sanding. Anyone who has stroked (and stroked) the rolling dunes of a Windsor chair seat, navigated endless valleys of crown molding or surrendered to the paint-clogged crevices of a double-hung window has surely prayed for divine assistance (or at least an electric gizmo).

That's why most wood shops resemble a sanding Circus McGurkus of motorized big belts, small pads and spinning discs, of sanders that orbit, vibrate and whirl, of hissing air-powered ones and angled, sucking and muscle-bound benchtop ones. Well, here's another for the troupe, a handheld power tool that looks like a platypus, hums like barber's clippers and makes short work of smoothing small spaces: the detail sander.

Unlike bigger sanders, detail sanders have a ferret's talent for nosing into awkward places. Often called corner sanders (for the tight spots they reach) or triangle sanders (for their distinctive pads), they're the sports cars of sanding: nimble and quick in sharp turns but hardly the right ride for heavy hauling. Detail sanders get the best chance to strut and stroke during remodeling work. Tom Silva has two, and though they don't get nearly as much use as his other sanders, they're "definitely handy," he says.

Before the first detail sander came along in 1987, an orbital palm sander was about the only motorized recourse for sanding into corners. Unfortunately, its square pad couldn't reach all the way in without shivering feverishly against adjacent cliffs. The points of a detail sander's triangular pad meet at less than 90 degrees so they slip easily into corners and along edges. With his detail sanders, Tom can smooth every nuance of a staircase newel, then slip between balusters to sand steps and, finally, work the edges of a riser without chattering against the skirtboard. "They're also great," he says, "for sanding window trim and touching up the corners of windowsills or edging floors right up to the baseboard to clean up where bigger sanders missed."

And In This Corner: A svelte body and a nose for tight spaces take detail sanders where other power sanders won't go. 1. The Pinocchio-like pad typical of most models projects forward so the tool body won't bump woodwork, making it ideal for sanding where tread, riser and skirtboard meet. 2. The tiny teeth on the slender saw blade attached to this sander can slice through chair spindles or plunge cut through standing baseboard. The blade doesn't spin; it oscillates at high speed. 3. A hard wool-felt pad dosed with buffing compound returns the gleam to old hardware. The triangular pad can reach places a standard buffer might not. 4. Fitted with a scraping blade, the oscillating motion of a detail sander can peel off decades of caked radiator paint.

Corner Specialist

Pinpoint Slicer

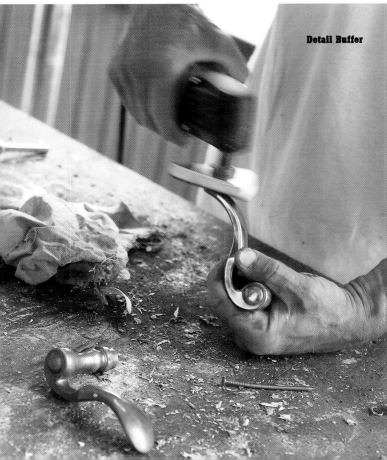
Detail Buffer

Scale Scraper

[detail sanders]

ORBITAL: Rechargeable batteries offer mobility. This slender single-speed tool is best for occasional use. Hook-and-loop abrasive. (5,000 opm)

IN-LINE: A variable-speed machine durable enough for prolonged use. Solid-rubber profiles. PSA abrasive. (2,100 to 6,000 spm)

OSCILLATING: This tough tool was the first detail sander; it now has electronic variable speed control and a host of attachments. Hook-and-loop or PSA abrasive. (12,000 to 21,000 spm)

ORBITAL: A gear-driven model with soft-grip top, through-pad dust pickup and variable-speed control. Hook-and-loop abrasive. (13,000 to 19,000 opm)

IN-LINE: Compact and lightweight. Uses hollow rubber profiles with easy-to-rotate non-adhesive sanding sleeves. (4,000 to 8,500 spm)

SANDER-PAD ROTATION DIRECTION

OSCILLATING (SPM = STROKES PER MINUTE)

ORBITAL (OPM = ORBITS PER MINUTE)

IN-LINE (SPM = STROKES PER MINUTE)

QUARTER-SHEET ORBITAL PAD SANDERS such as this one are the closest cousins to detail sanders. The square pad puts more abrasive on the job but can't reach all the places a detail sander can. Speed, in orbits per minute, is comparable to the detail-sander crowd.

ORBITAL: Gear-driven, with variable-speed controls. Includes dust port and slide-lock switch. Hook-and-loop abrasive. (7,000 to 11,000 opm)

OSCILLATING: Inexpensive sander for home use has two speeds, optional dust-collection tube and slender grip. PSA abrasive. (9,000 and 12,000 spm)

[detail sanders]

a detailer
*can be tricky
to control. Tom's tip:
ease into the action
by letting the sander
reach full speed
before touching it to
the work.*

Most detail sanders have bodies that wrap around a heavy-duty motor, making them as awkward to hold one-handed as a bottle of cabernet. "You won't want to hang onto it for a long time," admits Tom, but that's rarely necessary anyway—the task, after all, is sanding details, not plywood sheets. Slender sanders are easier to hold, but their smaller motors aren't up to a tough slog on the job site. Dust ports for an optional vacuum hose are a useful feature for production work, but detail sanders kick up so little sawdust that Tom rarely wrestles with a hose unless he's sanding paint or the adhesive squeeze-out on a solid-surface countertop.

Having hand sanded details for years, most craftsmen still have the habit of folding or wrapping sandpaper around a scrap block or a dowel. It's a low-tech approach that works fine, albeit slowly. When the road ahead is long and winding, though, or if patience isn't your virtue, a detail sander beats scraps of grit and a box of Band-Aids any day.

There are three kinds of detail sanders. A thorough detail sanding, like a hot tango, takes two: an oscillating or orbital to handle the flats, an in-line for the curves.

Oscillating detail sanders have a triangular sanding pad mounted on a spindle that jitters back and forth at up to 12,000 strokes per minute (spm). If the spindle is attached to one side of the sanding pad, the whole pad pivots back and forth like a high-speed windshield wiper; if it's attached at the center, the pad twists like Chubby Checkers. Either way, the greatest movement—and the greatest wear—is at the tips of the pad. Oscillating sanders inevitably sand across wood grain, though the minuscule distance traveled by the pad (and

evolution of a tool

THE MUSCLE-BOUND METRONOME WE CALL A DETAIL SANDER BEGAN LIFE AS A SEALANT SLICER IN STUTTGART, GERMANY. MERCEDES-BENZ WAS ATTEMPTING IN 1983 TO MOUNT ITS WINDSHIELDS IN POLYURETHANE, BUT THE EXPERIMENT WORKED ALL TOO WELL; ONCE THE SEALANT STUCK, IT CLUNG SO TENACIOUSLY THAT REPLACING THE GLASS WAS NEXT TO IMPOSSIBLE. SO MERCEDES TURNED TO THE FEIN TOOL CO. FEIN CREATED AN OSCILLATING TOOL THAT SWUNG A KNIFE THROUGH 21,000 TINY ARCS A MINUTE, NEATLY PARTING GLASS FROM RUBBER. THE SAME MOTION PUTS THE BUZZ INTO A BARBER'S CLIPPERS AND THE HOOTCHIE-COOTCHIE INTO TOOLS THAT RAKE OUT THE GROUT BETWEEN BRITTLE TILES. SURGEONS HAVE OSCILLATING SAWS TO MAKE SKULL CUTS; ORTHOPEDISTS USE THEM TO SAFELY SLICE OFF CASTS (THE BLADE BURROWS NEATLY THROUGH ANY HARD, UNYIELDING SURFACE, BUT WON'T CUT SKIN, WHICH WIGGLES HARMLESSLY IN SYNCH WITH EACH STROKE).

FEIN FINALLY ADAPTED THE TOOL TO THE CONSTRUCTION INDUSTRY, ADDING AN ARSENAL OF ACCESSORIES THAT CAN POLISH METAL, SLICE WOOD, VIBRATE CONCRETE AND FINISH-SAND CORNERS. NOW EUROPEAN CONTRACTORS CONSIDER THE TOOL AS A JOB SITE NECESSITY. IN THE UNITED STATES, HOWEVER, CONTRACTORS GENERALLY REGARD THE TOOL AS JUST A SPECIALIZED SANDER THAT CAN FREELANCE AT A FEW OTHER TASKS.

BELT DRIVE: The relatively small motor in this battery-powered sander allows it to be placed at a 90-degree angle to the tool's body, an arrangement that allows a slender, easily grasped handle. A quiet, toothed, fiberglass-reinforced belt links the drive gear (located at the end of the motor) to the orbiting mechanism.

GEAR DRIVE: This sander has a sturdy pinion-and-bevel-gear drive. An eccentric driveshaft fits into a bearing on the back of the sanding pad; as the bearing orbits, so does the pad. The shaft is fitted with counterweights to reduce vibration. To make room for all this, the motor ends up in the handle of the tool.

PIVOT DRIVE: The wiggle of this sander's pad starts with a simple bend in the motor's armature shaft (bottom of photo). A bearing secured to the shaft orbits in a tight circle, pushing back and forth a steel yoke forged to the sanding pad's shaft. The connection is elegantly straightforward, very durable and virtually unstoppable.

the proper technique) minimizes scratching. "Use fine sandpaper, move the sander slowly and use a light touch," Tom says.

Orbital detail sanders look just like their oscillating cousins, but the pad orbits in tight circles at up to 13,000 orbits per minute (opm). This action is less likely to leave cross-grain scratches but can chatter on curved surfaces, making it tricky to control. About the only way to tell an oscillating detail sander from an orbital model is to look for an spm or opm speed listing on the motor plate.

Shinnied up an entirely different branch of the detailer family tree is the in-line detail sander. Instead of oscillating or orbiting, the pad moves in a linear fashion back and forth

at speeds (up to 6,000 spm) that would burn calluses off the hardiest hand sander. These in-line workhorses rely on a battalion of hollow or solid rubber "profiles," each wrapped with pressure-sensitive adhesive (PSA) paper or tucked into a sanding sleeve, to sand dusty trails over hill and dale. Solid profiles won't deform when pressed hard and can be whittled to fit unusual shapes. Hollow-rubber profiles are more flexible than solid profiles and easier to load with sandpaper.

Whatever the sander type, Tom wants his to accept fuzzy-backed hook-and-loop papers. Unlike PSA sandpaper, hook-and-loop paper can be pulled off and repositioned in an instant when one gets scoured gritless.

[drills]

Plugged into steady, limitless

power and accessorized to suit any situation,

AN ELECTRIC DRILL TURNS INTO AN EVER-READY COMPANION WITH the muscular versatility of a decathlete and the heart of a seasoned long-distance runner. It can wrestle 6-inch holes through joists, vault up and over obstructions and run longer than you can in any remodeling marathon. Fit with all manner of accessories to mix, grind and scour, a corded drill is ready for any opponent . . . including Tom Silva. When he had to drill bolt holes through a triple-decker flitch beam sandwich (two all-steel patties of ½-inch sheet between buns of laminated veneer lumber), he didn't grab a cordless drill. "A big hole or a lot of 'em," says Tom, "and a cordless won't do."

CLAW: Riddled with tiny ragged craters, a hollow drum can cut wood in either direction.

The first pistol-grip electric drill, invented by Duncan Black and Alonzo Decker in 1916, spun a ½-inch chuck at 600 rpm, weighed 21½ pounds and required two men to operate. Pulling the trigger switch stopped the tool. This is not, however, the world's oldest electric drill. That title belongs to a squat 16½-pounder created in 1895 by Fein, a German company then in the business of making fire alarms. Fein's drill looked more like a carriage lantern than a power tool.

[drills]

In the century or so since the first electric models appeared, drills have evolved into a bewildering variety of types, styles and sizes. A visit to a tool store or a cruise through catalogs turns up prices ranging from $40 to more than $200. Why a drill costs what it does and how well it performs depends on its innards: its gearing, bearings and motor construction. But short of taking one apart, the best way to judge a drill's construction is to look at its chuck size and speed rating.

Chucks are measured by the largest diameter shank they accept: $\frac{1}{4}$ inch, $\frac{3}{8}$ inch (the most common) and $\frac{1}{2}$ inch. Drills of the two larger sizes are standard these days, and only a few companies still make the light, maneuverable $\frac{1}{4}$-inch drills that were once ubiquitous. The particular popularity of the $\frac{3}{8}$-inch chuck stems from the fact that it is reasonably light yet big enough to handle many spade bits and drill accessories. Keyless hand-tightened chucks are particularly popular in this size.

Tom, however, prefers a $\frac{1}{2}$-inch chuck with a key, the setup on nearly all of his half-dozen corded drills. "It just doesn't make sense to use anything less," he explains. It takes a lot of torque (turning force) to spin the fat shanks on the attachments he uses—everything from big auger bits to mortar-mixing paddles —and a $\frac{1}{2}$-inch chuck generally indicates robust inner workings that are up to the task.

How fast the chuck turns always involves a trade-off between speed and torque: The more of one, the less of the other. Most general utility drills run at a top speed of about 1,200 revolutions per minute. Drills designed for heavier-duty work have motors geared down to 900 rpm or so. And when the going really gets tough, top speed will be 300 to 600 rpm. Using these slow spinners, plumbers hog holes

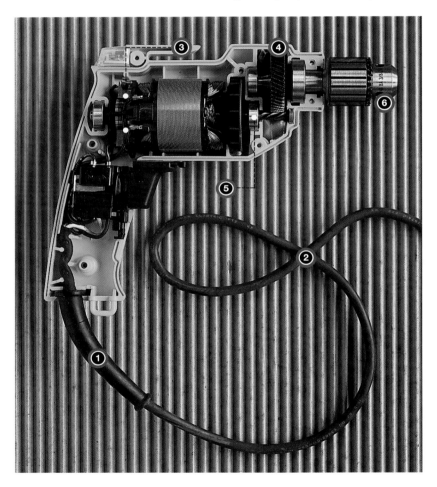

A Good Drill Undressed: Will a drill stand up to hard use? The answer is yes, if it has such features as these: 1. A cord-protecting strain-relief fitting reinforces the power cord right where the cord is most vulnerable (at the handle). 2. A rubber cord jacket is more flexible and wear resistant than a plastic jacket. 3. Auto-stop motor brushes won't get stuck in the motor when they wear down to nubbins, and thus avoid a potentially expensive repair—or the need for an entirely new drill. 4. Helical gearing is stronger and more efficient than spur gears. 5. Ball or needle bearings are smoother and longer lasting than bronze bushings. Some drills use a combination of bushings and bearings. 6. A keyed chuck with precisely ground jaws affords the best grip.

through framing lumber and drywall crews mix 5-gallon batches of joint compound.

All corded drills have a chuck and a trigger switch, but that's about where the similiarities end. Handles, for instance, come in the familiar pistol grip, the T (which balances the motor's weight over the hand), the D (which puts the hand in line with the motor) and the spade (a D handle turned 90 degrees that's often adjustable). Choosing one over another is partly a matter of comfort. Double-insulated drills have plastic housings and two-prong plugs; drills with metal housings need three-prong grounding. Amperage (listed on the spec plate) is a rough guide to a tool's power, but the rarely used "watts out" is more accurate.

The most durable drills have machined parts (more precise than cast steel), high-efficiency motors (more output for a given amperage input), extra-thick insulation on the motor windings (more protection against short circuits), externally-accessible motor brushes (for easy replacment) and bearing-supported motor shafts. On shock-resistant double-insulated drills, housings of glass-reinforced nylon resist impact and solvents better than polycarbonate. Keyless chucks with a steel shell wear better than chucks with a shell of glass-filled nylon.

But no drill can win Tom's affection unless he likes the way it feels in his hand. "If I have to spend the whole day with it," he explains, "the right one won't leave me tired."

GRIND: For smoothing edges and working metal down to size, a coarse-grit wheel has no equal.

BRUSH: Stiff metal bristles scour rust from metal surfaces, but they're far too tough to work wood.

SCALE: Legions of sharp metal scales march into small holes in wood to make them bigger.

WHIRL: Stiff nylon fingers infused with a fine abrasive reach into cracks and crevices to remove paint.

"IT'S THE BIT THAT MAKES THE DRILL LOOK GOOD," SAYS TOM, AND PERHAPS THAT'S WHY SO MANY BITS (AND ACCESSORIES) ARE AVAILABLE. WHENEVER HE PICKS UP A BIT, HE LOOKS FOR NICKS, ROUNDED EDGES AND THE BLUE DISCOLORATION INDICATING LOST TEMPER. THEN HE GRAZES HIS FINGERTIPS OVER THE BIT'S EDGES TO TEST SHARPNESS. "IF IT'S NOT IN GOOD SHAPE, I WON'T USE IT," HE SAYS. EVEN THE SHARPEST BITS MAKE SPLINTERY EXITS, SO TOM CLAMPS A SCRAP BEHIND THE HOLE. HIGH-TORQUE DRILLS WILL GET THE JUMP ON INATTENTIVE DRILLERS, A FACT TOM KNOWS ALL TOO WELL. ONCE WHEN A KNOT STOPPED A BIT COLD, THE DRILL SWUNG COUNTERCLOCKWISE AND CARRIED HIS HAND THROUGH THE ADJACENT DRYWALL BEFORE HE COULD RELEASE THE TRIGGER. NOW HE ALWAYS BRACES HIMSELF WITH A WIDE STANCE AND USES AN AUXILIARY HANDLE.

AN ELECTRIC DRILL ISN'T JUST FOR MAKING HOLES, HOWEVER. JUST ABOUT ANY OBJECT THAT CAN BE STUCK ON A SPINDLE HAS BEEN CHUCKED INTO A DRILL, MAKING IT INTO A TOOL THAT WILL REMOVE OR SMOOTH ANY SURFACE. BUT WHATEVER RESIDUE IS SPUN OFF INVARIABLY DEMANDS ONE ADDITIONAL—AND ESSENTIAL —DRILL ACCESSORY: A GOOD PAIR OF SAFETY GLASSES (SEE PAGE 94).

SAND: An abrasive sleeve wrapped over a rubber drum smooths or strips paint from curved edges.

WHIP: Paint disappears as hinged bristles thrash wood without harming it.

drill team

[drills]

A Family Portrait: Members of the corded-drill family all spin chucks both clockwise (for drilling and screwing) and counterclockwise (for screw removal). Nonetheless, they otherwise exhibit a surprising amound of diversity. Handles, for example, come in the familiar pistol grip (3,4,6,8), the T (11), the D (5,7), and the spade (2, 10) versions, as well as other configurations (1, 9). Double-insulated drills have plastic housings and two-prong plugs; metal housings require a three-prong plug for grounding.

1. A compact ⅜-inch drill with a paddle switch reaches places other drills can't.
2. The removable auxiliary handle provides extra leverage to resist this ½-inch drill's high torque.

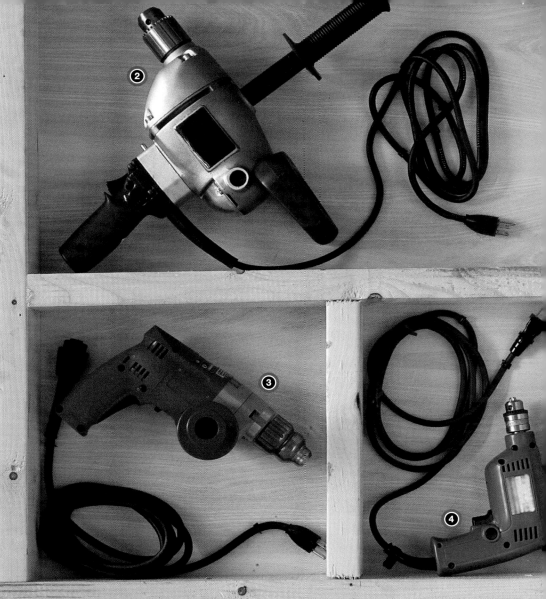

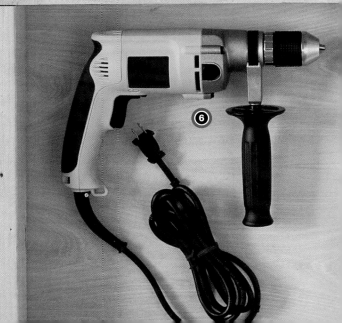

3. Ratcheting action lets the keyless ½-inch chuck of this drill bite down hard on bits. 4. This ¼-inch drill weighs a mere 2 pounds; many other pistol-grip drills weigh at least twice that amount. 5. A depth stop comes standard on this D-handled model. 6. Can't get the keyless ½-inch chuck tight enough? Push a button to lock this drill's spindle. 7. The long housing and sturdy D handle of this ½-inch right-angle drill help the user resist its torque. 8. A powerful permanent-magnet motor powers this mighty ½-inch mite that's smaller than most other ½-inch pistol-grip drills. A loop on the strain-relief fitting is for a chuck key.

9. If this slim right-angle drill and its ⅜-inch chuck can't reach into a space, you probably can't drill there. 10. Three handles cope with this ½-inch drill's weight and torque. 11. This ⅜-inch T-handled drill has a one-piece cast-aluminum handle and housing.

[drills]

IT TAKES A LOT OF WORK TO MAKE A LITTLE BIT. BEHIND EVERY DRILL bit is a complex process that turns raw steel into a precision instrument. The path from billet to bit begins with clean steel, free of contaminants such as sulphur which weaken the cutting edge. At the factory, bits are forged from steel bars in the hell of the hammer shop. There, after a piece is heated to 1,700 degrees Fahrenheit and sandwiched between forging dies, huge trip-hammers pound the dies together to form the basic shape. The alternative to forging is investment casting, in which a mold is built up around a wax bit. When molten metal is poured in, the wax melts and is replaced by steel.

BIT PARTS

BRAD POINT: Sharp point; keeps bit from wandering when a hole is started.

LIP OR KNIFE: Sharpened edge between point and spurs; cuts hole bottom.

GULLET: Where lip feeds chips to the flutes. If it clogs, drilling stops.

SPUR: Edge that scores and severs wood fibers to create the hole's wall.

FLUTE: Helical groove winding around the shank of a twist drill.

LAND: Flat band winding around extremities of a bit's flute.

WEB: Metal at the base of the flute that forms the core of the bit.

After forging or casting, rough-formed bits must cool, though not too quickly or the steel becomes brittle. Then, after a quick tumble in silica or another abrasive to remove flakes of metal and oxides, computers take over. They control mills and lathes that refine the basic shape into a high-tolerance piece. To pass muster at some factories, the concentricity (roundness) of a 1-inch diameter bit must be within .0002 inch of a perfect circle.

More heat-treating follows to control the metal's hardness. Then, for some bits, people take over for a task that computers haven't mastered, using grinders to hone the cutting edges to near razor sharpness. For the trip to the store, the bits are protected in plastic pouches and wooden cases. In the hands of their new owners, they still need that protection—the worst thing you can possibly do is just throw them in a drawer.

Despite their differing shapes and uses, drill bits have essentially the same anatomy. In the elegant physics of making a hole, cutting edges bore in, and twisting flutes lift out shavings, chips and dust. And whatever the bit, the right steel is what makes it worth having. Good steel comes from Europe, Scandinavia, America and Japan. Recipes for bit steel vary with the end use: Woodworking rarely needs anything harder than chrome-vanadium steel. Boring metal requires high-speed steel, which has more chromium and molybdenum so the tip won't lose its temper in the high heat of drilling. Oddly, that recipe can be defeated by plastic and particleboard. Those materials require steel with tungsten carbide, which hardens the steel an additional 30 percent.

[drills]

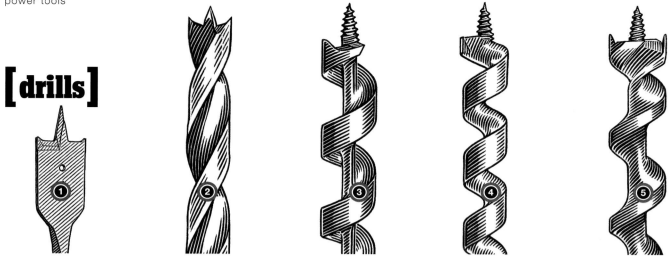

WOOD BITS

1. Spade Bit: Inexpensive and disposable bit that scrapes instead of cuts. It's best for rough work because it can't make as clean and straight a hole as a brad point. Diameter: $\frac{1}{4}$" to $1\frac{1}{2}$". Length: 7", 16". **2. Brad-Point Twist Drill:** With a point that keeps it centered and spurs that sever the fibers, this bit drills cleanly and accurately and is good for dowelling. Diameter: $\frac{1}{8}$" to 1". Length: $2\frac{3}{4}$" to 6"; also available extralong to 12". **3. Single Cutter, Solid-Center Auger:** For use with a hand brace or power drill, the screw tip pulls the cutting lip into wood. Large auger clears chips quickly, wide lands stabilize bit. Diameter: $\frac{1}{4}$" to $1\frac{1}{2}$" Length: $7\frac{1}{2}$". **4. Single Cutter, Hollow-Center Auger:** Side lips and hollow center clear chips fast. Drills deep holes in poles and timbers. Also called ship auger or l'Hommedieu pattern. Diameter: $\frac{1}{4}$" to $1\frac{1}{2}$". Length: $7\frac{1}{2}$", 12", 18", 29". **5. Double Cutter, Solid-Center Auger:** Twin spurs and lips cut a cleaner hole than single-cutter augers. Also called Irwin pattern. Diameter: $\frac{1}{4}$" to $1\frac{1}{2}$". Length: $7\frac{1}{2}$", 12", 18".

GLOSSARY

AIRCRAFT-LENGTH: Extralong twist drills, commonly 6 and 12 inches. So named because they're favored by metalworkers in the aircraft industry. AUGER: The helical shaft of a wood-cutting bit, along which the chips eject. BRACE: A hand-operated crank that holds and drives an auger bit into wood. CENTER PUNCH: A pointed tool for making a tiny dimple in metal to locate a drill bit and help to start the hole. CLEARANCE HOLE: A hole drilled the same size as the outside diameter of the threads on a screw, which allows them to pass through the piece unimpeded.

WOOD BITS

6. Multispur Bit: A Forstner bit with a sawtooth rim that allows for quicker and cooler cutting. For use in a drill press only. Diameter: $\frac{1}{4}$" to 4". Length: $3\frac{1}{2}$". **7. Two-Piece Spade Bit:** Threaded shank accepts any diameter cutting head, which has a replaceable screw point for power drills and a replaceable brad point for drill presses. Diameter: 1" to 5". Length: $3\frac{1}{2}$", $5\frac{1}{2}$", 12", 18". **8. Bellhanger Bit:** Long enough to reach through walls and floors to aid in running telephone wire and TV cable (entire length not shown here). Choose one with a small hole in web for pulling wire back through the hole. Diameter: $\frac{3}{16}$" to $\frac{1}{2}$". Length: 12", 18", 24", 30". **9. Screw-Point Multispur Bit:** The true plumber's friend, this wood eater pulls itself through studs and joists. Sized for pipes and electrical conduit and has a replaceable screw center. Diameter: 1" to $4\frac{5}{8}$". Length: $3\frac{1}{2}$". **10. Screw-Point Spade Bit:** Designed primarily for running electrical wire and conduit, this bit is self-feeding in tight stud and joist bays. Diameter: $\frac{1}{2}$" to $1\frac{1}{2}$". Length: 6".

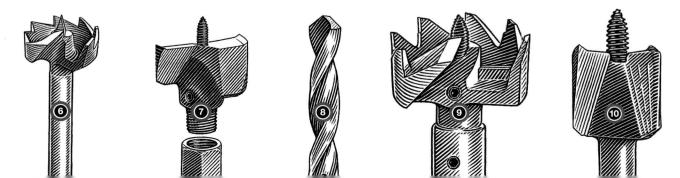

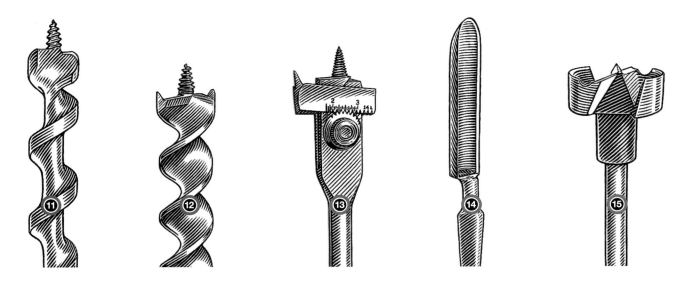

WOOD BITS

11. Sugar-Tapping Auger: Made for tapping sap from sugar maples. The center screw pulls bit into the wood. To minimize injury to the tree, the auger has no spurs. Diameter: $7/16$". Length: 6". **12. Double-Twist Auger:** Smaller lands help keep the bore straight and reduce friction. Also called Jennings pattern. Diameter: $1/4$" to $1\frac{1}{2}$". Length: 6" to 8". **13. Adjustable Bit:** This classic hand-brace bit works best when really sharp, though the single-spur design can't cut a precision hole. Drill-press versions are also available. Diameter: $5/8$" to $1\frac{3}{4}$", $7/8$" to 3", $7/8$" to 5". Length: $5\frac{1}{2}$" to 8". **14. Chair-Maker's Spoon Bit:** Drills tapered holes for chair legs and spindles, and holes that are wider inside than at the opening, which aids in joining spindles to seats. Diameter: $3/8$" to $3/4$". Length: $2\frac{1}{2}$". **15. Forstner Bit:** This smoothest of wood-boring bits is the cabinetmaker's favorite. The whole rim is a cutting spur, so the bit makes clean, flat-bottomed holes. Best used in a drill press, though brad-point versions can be used in a portable electric drill. Diameter: $1/4$" to 3". Length: $3\frac{1}{2}$" to $10\frac{1}{2}$".

COBALT STEEL: An exceptionally hard and heat-resistant tool steel; more durable than high-speed steel. COUNTER-BORE: A shallow hole larger than the head of a screw, bolt or washer. Permits setting the head below the surface of the workpiece. COUNTERSINK: A conical hole the same shape as the head of an oval or flathead screw. Allows head to be set flush with the surface. CUTTING OIL: Lubricates and thus minimizes the heat of friction when drilling metal or glass; also floats away shavings and chips. DRILL GAUGE: Metal plate with labeled holes for checking the diameter of twist drills.

WOOD BITS

16. Cornering Spade Bit: Round-shouldered bit can be steered through a 45-degree turn to aid in snaking electrical wire around corners. Diameter: $7/8$", $1\frac{1}{8}$". Length: $6\frac{1}{4}$". **17. Pocket-Hole Step Drill:** Drilling a shallow-angle hole for panhead screws is a quick way to join the stiles and rails of cabinet face frames. It works best with a pocket-hole guide. Diameter: $1/8$" tip, $3/8$" shaft. Length: 5".

METAL AND PLASTIC BITS

18. 118-Degree Point Twist Drill: A workhorse bit that can make any size hole in metal but only small holes in wood. Diameter: .0135" to .2280" (wire gauge 80 to 1), .2340" to .4130" (letter size A to Z), $1/64$" to 1" (fractional inch). Length: $3/4$" to 6". **19. 135-degree Split-Point Twist Drill:** Self-centers in metal and doesn't require use of a center punch. Diameter and Length: same as 118-degree point. **20. 60-Degree Point Twist Drill:** Patented point design that drills more efficiently and stays sharp longer. Diameter: $1/16$" to $1/2$". Length: up to 6".

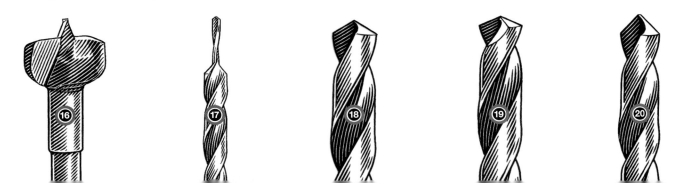

[drills]

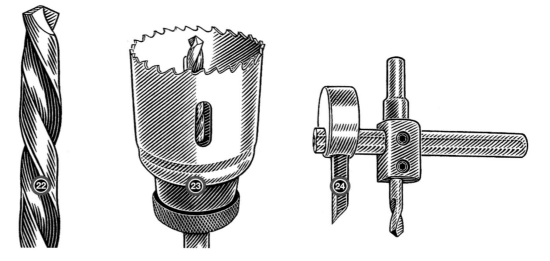

SPECIALTY BITS

21. Hollow-Chisel Mortising Bit: Mounted on a drill press, spinning bit cuts the bottom of a mortise while the hollow chisel squares the corners (chisel does not spin). Diameter: $\frac{1}{4}$" to 1". Length: 9". **22. Left-Handed Twist Drill:** For use in reversible drills and drill presses. Can help extract broken bolts and studs. Diameter: .0135" to .2280" (wire gauge 80 to 1), $\frac{1}{32}$" to $\frac{1}{2}$" (fractional inch). Length: up to 6". **23. Holesaw:** Interchangeable saws fit onto a mandrel with a twist-drill center. Best for large, through holes in wood, as when installing locksets and running pipes. Diameter: $\frac{9}{16}$" to 6". Depth of cut: $1\frac{1}{8}$" to $1\frac{5}{8}$". **24. Adjustable Circle Cutter:** Centers with a twist drill and cuts a hole or a disk in thin wood, metal or plastic. Diameter: $\frac{7}{8}$" to 8". Maximum depth of cut: 1".

DRILL INDEX: Metal box that stores and sorts twist bits by size. FRACTIONAL TWIST DRILLS: Bits sized in increments of $\frac{1}{64}$ inch. HIGH-SPEED STEEL: Tungsten and molybdenum content allows it to remain hard at high temperatures and resist the frictional heat of drilling. Marked "HSS" on the drill shank.

JOBBER LENGTH: The standard length for twist drills. Depends on diameter and ranges from $\frac{3}{4}$-inch long for $\frac{1}{64}$ inch bits to 6 inches for 1 inch bits. PILOT HOLE: A hole drilled the same size as the root or core diameter of threads on a screw. PIN VISE: A drill chuck that holds very small bits. Can be rotated

SPECIALTY BITS

25. Drywall Side-Cutter: Flutes cut holes in drywall for electrical-box installation. Diameter: $\frac{1}{8}$". Length: $2\frac{1}{4}$". **26. Multipurpose Bit:** Faceted split-point carbide tip drills through metal, masonry, plastic and wood. Diameter: $\frac{1}{8}$" to $\frac{1}{2}$". Length: 3" to 6. **27. Nonadjustable Drill and Countersink:** In one move, drills accurate clearance and pilot holes and also countersinks for screw heads. Diameter: $\frac{1}{8}$" to $\frac{1}{4}$" (for #5 to #14 wood screws). Length: $\frac{3}{4}$" to 2". **28. Adjustable Tapered Drill And Countersink:** Drills clearance holes, pilot holes and countersinks. Can be adjusted for screws of different lengths. Diameter: $\frac{5}{64}$" to $\frac{3}{8}$" (for #2 to #24 wood screws). Length: $1\frac{11}{16}$" to $3\frac{1}{8}$". **29. Vix Self-Centering Bit:** A retractable bit in a spring-loaded sleeve automatically centers itself in predrilled screw holes of hinges. Diameter: $\frac{5}{64}$" to $\frac{13}{64}$" (#3 to #14 wood screws). Maximum depth of cut: 1" to $1\frac{1}{2}$".

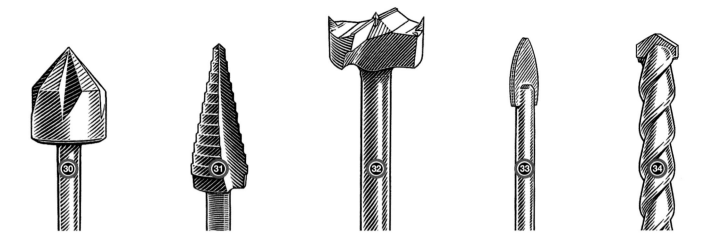

30. **Rose Countersink:** 82-degree cutter has lips to scrape out the seat for a screw head in metal, plastic or wood. Diameter: $\frac{1}{4}$" to 1". 31. **Step Drill:** Able to make a dozen different size holes in sheet metal and other thin materials. Diameter: $\frac{3}{8}$" to $1\frac{1}{8}$". Step depth: $\frac{1}{8}$". 32. **Carbide-Tipped Four-Wing Bit:** Designed for plastic laminate, fiberboard and other abrasive materials. Diameter: $\frac{1}{2}$" to $2\frac{1}{2}$". Length: 6". Maximum depth of cut: 1". 33. **Spear-Point Bit:** Carbide point can grind a hole in glass, tile or other hard, brittle materials. Diameter: $\frac{1}{8}$" to $\frac{1}{2}$". Length: 3" to 5", depending on diameter. 34. **Masonry Bit:** Broad carbide tip chews into concrete, brick or mortar. This bit is best used with a hammer drill. Diameter: $\frac{1}{8}$" to 1". Length: 3" to 13".

between the fingers to make a hole. PLUG CUTTER: Hollow-center bit cuts wood plugs for filling holes, such as over screws set below the surface. SHANK EXTENSION: A rod with a socket that holds and extends the reach and/or depth of a drill bit. Not for use in a drill press. STOP COLLAR: Metal or plastic ring fastened onto a drill bit to limit the depth of the hole. TITANIUM NITRIDE AND ZIRCONIUM NITRIDE: Electronically deposited drill-bit coatings that greatly increase hardness. TUNGSTEN CARBIDE: A hard, brittle material used to make abrasion-resistant points for drills and other cutting tools.

TYPES OF BIT SHANKS

When it comes to choosing the right drill bit to suit a particular situation (and a particular drill), pay attention to the shank as well as to the point. Bits with a round shank (1), a reduced round shank (2), or a hex-sided shank (3) can be used with power drills and drill presses. Round-shank bits are the ones most commonly used in portable drills. Reduced round shank bits enable large-diameter bits to fit in relatively small chucks. Hex-shank bits are less prone than round-shank bits to slip under heavy loads. Bits with tapered square shanks (4) are suitable only for use in an auger brace. Some auger bits have a combination tapered-square and hex shank (5). On these, the tapered square portion can be sawn off to make the bit suitable for power drilling.

[electricplanes]

An electric plane, to one who knows it,

may be far less mysterious than a hand plane.

A NOVICE COUNTS A HAND PLANE AS A PUZZLE OF LEVERS AND KNOBS that either plows up great slivers or refuses to cut at all. Rather than rely on such a tool to shave the swelled edges of a door, many homeowners let their doors stick. By contrast, an electric power plane makes the job easy. A turn of its calibrated knob sets the blade depth faultlessly. And with a pair of blades spinning about 15,000 times a minute, the plane takes all the elbow grease out of wood removal; just hold it steady as you slide it over the wood.

CUTTING GUARD: Swings aside so the tool can cut grooves up to ½- inch deep or clean out the corners of rabbets.

DEPTH-OF-CUT KNOB: Twists to raise or lower front shoe, setting cutting depth from $\frac{1}{64}$ to $\frac{1}{8}$ inch. Doubles as a guide handle.

TRIGGER SWITCH: Turns the plane on and off.

CHIP DISCHARGE CHUTE: Removes debris sliced off by the blades.

HEEL: Flips up during cuts; drops down to support end of a resting plane, preventing damage to exposed blades.

REAR SHOE: Limits depth of cut. A long rear shoe makes it easier to hold the tool steady.

BLADES: Also called knives, they're usually self-aligning and made of carbide; replace in pairs to ensure uniform cuts.

CUTTING CYLINDER: Belt-driven cylinder holds two blades and spins at 12,000 to 19,000 rpm, depending on make.

FRONT SHOE: Height determines depth of cut; grooves steady the tool when cutting chamfers.

The earliest power planes, introduced in the late 1970s, had motors that hung below the shoe on one side, making them just about useless for planing anything but the narrow edges of wooden doors. Now that motors live above the shoe, planes are free to flatten wide expanses of wood. The models that smooth swaths 3¼-inches wide are the most popular. Carpenters use them to flatten bowed joists so that subfloors will lie flat. Makers of solid-surface countertops, for bathrooms and kitchens, use them to remove hardened glue squeezed out of seams.

[powerplanes]

Timber framers rely on larger models that range from 6 inches to a full foot in width to fine-tune the joints in giant beams or put a fresh surface on salvaged timbers. One model even has a flexible shoe that allows stair builders, boatbuilders and even surfboard makers to follow concave or convex curves. And cabinet-makers who want to trim an applied edge perfectly flush with the adjoining surface have a lipper/plane, which has a cutting arm that adjusts to make bevels.

Compared with belt sanders, another tool used for smoothing and removing wood, a power plane is faster and more precise. Once the cutting depth is set on a plane's adjustable front shoe, the fixed rear shoe prevents the blades from digging any deeper into the wood. Belt sanders also rough up wood and clog its pores with dust; a planer slices wood cleanly, leaving it smooth and particle-free. "Especially for gluing, when you need two perfectly matched pieces of wood for as tight a joint as possible, you want to plane the surface rather than sand it," says Tom Silva.

As easy as they are to use, however, power planes aren't foolproof. "The biggest mistake is to try and go too fast," says Tom. Pushing a plane too quickly will leave chatter marks (an uneven washboard surface). Cutting too deeply strains the motor and rips loose knots out of the wood. And when a plane's front

« Especially for gluing, when you need two perfectly matched pieces of wood for as tight as a joint as possible, you want to plane the surface. »

the plane facts

WITH TWO BLADES ZIPPING AROUND AT 250 TIMES PER SECOND, POWER PLANES CAN INSTANTLY MUTILATE POWER CORDS, WOOD AND FINGERS. FOLLOW THESE STEPS FOR SMOOTH, AND SAFE, OPERATION: 1. PROTECT YOUR HEARING WITH EARMUFFS OR PLUGS. SOME PLANERS ARE AS LOUD AS A LAWN MOWER. 2. INSPECT THE WOOD FIRST. A PRO-TRUDING NAIL CAN WRECK A BLADE, BUT SO CAN ORDINARY DIRT. 3. CUT IN SHALLOW PASSES. CUTTING TOO DEEP CAN BOG DOWN THE MOTOR, BURN OUT THE BRUSHES AND RIP UP THE WOOD. 4. PLANE IN THE DIRECTION OF THE GRAIN WITHOUT SKEWING THE TOOL. LIFT THE PLANE COMPLETELY OFF THE WOOD AT THE END OF EACH PASS TO PREVENT CUTTING BACKWARD, WHICH CHIPS THE WOOD. TOM SILVA ACTUALLY HAD A PLANE RIPPED OUT OF HIS HANDS WHEN HE DID THIS...ONCE. 5. AVOID THE CORD. WHEN PULLING THE PLANE BACK FOR THE NEXT PASS, IT'S EASY FOR THE BLADES TO CATCH THE CORD. LOOP THE CORD OVER YOUR SHOULDERS AND BEHIND YOUR NECK TO KEEP IT OUT OF HARM'S WAY.

TECHNIQUES

Curve Hugger: Timber framer Will Beemer uses a Spanish-made plane with a flexible steel shoe to smooth curves as well as flats. Here he tunes a concave cut that matches the timber braces (above) in his own house.

Hand Hewer: Beemer uses a power plane fitted with a curved blade to produce a convincing rough-hewn look (left). The same tool was used by timber framer Anthony Zaya to detail the trusses of a new house (above).

shoe slides off into thin air at the end of a cut, it's apt to dive and leave a telltale dip or snipe in the wood. Longer planes reduce the chance of snipe, but going slowly and holding the plane's rear shoe firmly against the work minimizes snipe on even the stubbiest models.

Another mistake you can make: Underestimating the storm of sawdust and wood chips that power planes unleash. That's why Tom works outdoors with his planes whenever possible. To rein in the deluge, some planes can be hooked up to a shop vacuum, but you better use a big one.

Sure, a hand plane can do what a power plane can, and you might even find it deeply soothing to curl up shavings with each slow stroke. But wouldn't you rather celebrate a victory over sticking doors by sending a satisfying spray of wood confetti into the air?

blades
get dull after about five hours of use; a laboring motor is the clue. Planing off paint increases wear, so Tom always scrapes by hand before he planes. Nothing, however, ruins a blade faster than hitting a nail.

[**extensioncords**]

AN EXTENSION CORD'S JOB SEEMS SO EASY— to convey electricity from here to there—that we hardly give the cord itself a second thought. But as electrician Paul J. Kennedy learned the hard way, any old tangle of wire won't do. About 20 years ago, the eager apprentice rigged a job-site extension cord from a 150-foot roll of standard household wire. Not much later, he recalls, "I knew something was wrong when I looked over and saw smoke." Kennedy remembers being pretty pleased with his ingenuity: a plug on either end of the wire, and it was ready to go. But within minutes, the wire got so hot its coating melted. His creation was on the verge of shorting out when he raced over to pull the plug. The physics of what went wrong are simple to understand: Kennedy tried to move too much power through too long a wire, turning it into something like the heating element on an electric stove. The still-coiled wire compounded his error by blocking the escape of heat. "I never did anything like that again," he says.

In-line circuit breakers cut the juice if loads exceed a preset amperage. Unlike GFCIs, they exist to protect wiring, not humans.

Tired of bending over to plug in different tools? On a cord with three outlets, a trio of tools can be ready to go all the time.

In the years since that near meltdown, the lowly extension cord has evolved into an advanced piece of equipment, with outer jackets that remain flexible in the coldest weather, plugs that light up when electricity is running through them, built-in circuit breakers, and plugs that lock together so well that a dangling cord and a powerless tool at the top of a ladder are things of the past.

« A cord's job seems so easy

Coiled and ready to strike, this extension cord has several desirable attributes. A three-pronged plug and a durable jacket made of old-fashioned natural rubber for maximum flexibility. The bright color is easy to find on a debris-strewn job site.

o convey electricity from here to there. »

[extension cords]

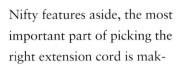

Nifty features aside, the most important part of picking the right extension cord is making sure it can safely deliver the power the tool at the other end needs. Whether a cord is right for the job depends on three things: how thick the wire is, how long it is and how many amperes of electricity will be drawn through it.

Gauge—the thickness of the wire inside a cord—determines how many amps a cord can handle. The thicker the wire, the *lower* the gauge and the more current it can carry. Ordinary household cords are typically 18- or 22-gauge wire—not at all suitable for workshops or job sites. Those environments require middleweight 14- and 16-gauge cords, which are fine for medium loads that don't have to travel very far. Outside, over distances of 50 feet or more, fat 10- and 12-gauge cords are the only way to go.

Length is a critical factor because even a good conductor like copper nibbles away at voltage. The longer the cord, the greater the voltage drop. A drop of 5 percent or more slows down a tool's motor, making it work harder, run hotter and die sooner. Kennedy's rules of thumb are: No cords longer than 150 feet—ever—and if different cords are plugged together, plug the heaviest gauge cord into the outlet.

When choosing an all-purpose cord, it's best to favor thicker wires and shorter lengths. The heat generated in undersized wire can permanently reduce copper's conductivity. For household and yard work, the total load on one cord shouldn't exceed 15 amps (the rating of a typical household circuit breaker). Any

The easier a cord coils up, the more likable it will be. Flexibility begins with the wire itself: the more strands per wire, the better. Seven strands are standard. Paper and plastic fillers allow wires to move inside the jacket and help maintain a round cross section. Most cords have PVC plastic jackets which get stiff in the cold. Rubber jackets don't; their flexibility is tops.

A short circuit in a tool or cord can kill you. Cords with a built-in ground-fault circuit interrupter (GFCI) eliminate the risk. Standard in bathroom outlets for years, GFCIs are newer additions on extension cords. When the device senses a tiny power surge–as low as 0.005 amp–it cuts off the power in $\frac{1}{40}$th of a second. An ordinary extension cord will administer a 120-volt jolt until the house circuit breaker cuts power. The interrupter should be plugged into a house outlet, never into another extension cord.

the lighter gauges—those with a third wire for grounding (as evidenced by a three-pronged plug) offer more protection in the event of a tool short circuit. Safer still are cords that include a ground-fault circuit interrupter (GFCI). You may have to hunt to find one, however, because even clerks at stores that cater to contractors don't always know what the things are and may suggest some other product that works "just as well." It won't.

Like many electricians, Kennedy has experienced—quite unintentionally—the full force of 120 volts. He shakes his head at the memory. "Don't go there," he says.

extension cord should bear UL (Underwriters' Laboratories) and OSHA (Occupational Safety and Health Administration) labeling on the package. And although many shop cords have two wires running through them—especially in

choosing an extension cord

TO CHOOSE THE RIGHT WIRE SIZE, FIRST DETERMINE THE AMP LOAD IT'S GOING TO CARRY. IF MORE THAN ONE TOOL WILL RUN ON THE SAME CORD AT THE SAME TIME, ADD ALL THE AMPS TOGETHER TO GET THE TOTAL LOAD. NEXT, DECIDE ON CORD LENGTH. THE CHART BELOW SHOWS THE MAXIMUM AMP LOAD AT A 3 PERCENT VOLTAGE DROP FOR THREE COMMON CORD LENGTHS. IF THE MAXIMUM AMPERAGE IS BETWEEN TWO WIRE GAUGES, USE THE THICKER ONE.

- ■ 10 Gauge
- ■ 12 Gauge
- ■ 14 Gauge
- ■ 16 Gauge

25 FEET OF CORD
- 15 amps
- 15 amps
- 15 amps
- 14 amps

50 FEET OF CORD
- 15 amps
- 15 amps
- 11 amps
- 7 amps

100 FEET OF CORD
- 14 amps
- 9 amps
- 5 amps
- 3 amps

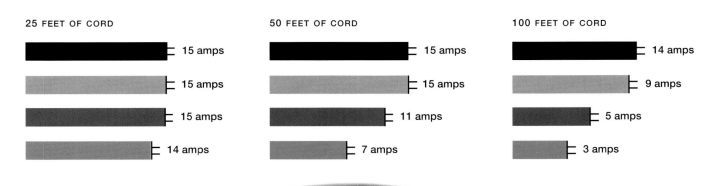

[**jigsaws**]

TOM SILVA'S SEVEN OR EIGHT JIGSAWS may gather dust for days before they make any, "but when we need one," says Tom, "we really need it." It's a tool of many names—saber saw, bayonet saw—and many uses. The short, stabbing, up-and-down motion of the blade enables a jigsaw to cut big sweeping curves and straight lines or nibble its way into tight corners. Tom grabs one when he must scribe trim to brick chimneys, fit cabinets to bowed walls, cut pipe, finish cuts made by circular saws or shape metal thresholds to doorjambs. The tool is invaluable for plunge-cutting holes for sinks, pipes and electrical outlets, and making decorative scrolls and shelf brackets—jobs where cutting finesse, not speed, is important.

Other tools can do similar work, but not as well. Reciprocating saws cut curves, but they're unruly for fine work. Circular saws cut through wood like it's butter, but only in straight lines. A handheld coping saw is precise but slow, and a band saw—though nearly as versatile as a jigsaw—isn't something to carry up a ladder. No wonder the little jigsaw is often the second power-tool purchase, after a drill, that a homeowner makes.

Though it may seem surprising, the biggest decision facing anyone buying a jigsaw is handle style. And on this point, jigsaw owners are deeply divided. European carpenters prefer to hold their saws by the barrel-shaped housing surrounding the motor. Americans, however, are equally fervent about the virtues of top-handled models. Tom? He's a barrel-grip guy: "A top-handle saw feels nice at first, but not once I start cutting. A barrel-grip saw

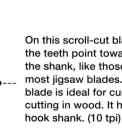

A high-speed steel blade cuts medium-weight metals and makes smooth cuts in wood. This one has a bayonet shank. (14 teeth per inch)

On this scroll-cut blade, the teeth point toward the shank, like those on most jigsaw blades. The blade is ideal for curve-cutting in wood. It has a hook shank. (10 tpi)

This is Tom's work-horse, an all-purpose, fast-cutting blade for wood. A universal shank is secured by one or two screws. (6 tpi)

This medium carbide-grit blade grinds through ceramic tile. Its wide body extends the cutting surface forward, permitting flush cuts.

The short, skinny blade of a jigsaw whips up and down 3,000 strokes per minute. A circular guide behind the blade helps to support it during cuts. Silva discards a blade the moment he suspects it's dull. "I gauge sharpness by the look of the teeth—sharp points and crisp edges." Check midblade, where most of the cutting happens. Be sure the replacement blade's shank is compatible with the saw (see photos at left).

VARIABLE-SPEED CONTROL: Adjust to get the smoothest cut. Not all are mounted on the on/off switch, as here.

QUICK-CHANGE CAP: Lift and turn to release the blade. Found only on a few models.

DUST PORT: Not on all saws.

ORBIT CONTROL: Adjusts orbit from off to agressive cutting. A smaller switch turns this saw's dust blower on and off.

CHANGEABLE SHOE: Cast aluminum adds stiffness; the steel insert can be swapped for plastic when cutting easily scratched materials, such as laminate.

RIP GUIDE: Saw fence (not shown) slips through hole, enabling the saw to make uniform rip or circle cuts.

1587DVS

SWISS MADE

seems more like an extension of my hand. When I move my hand, the saw just seems to follow along."

Jigsaws come in two price ranges. Simple models, fine for occasional use, go for less than $100. Professional-grade tools start at $130 or so and are more likely to include the features Tom prefers: variable-speed control; a stout, tilting shoe; a quick-change blade system that eliminates the need to hunt for an Allen wrench or a screwdriver; and orbital action. Orbital action swings the blade slightly forward on the upstroke, helping the saw cut more aggressively. An orbiting blade also makes better progress rounding tight turns; it clears more of a path for itself with each stroke, so it's less likely to bind. (For a clean cut and reduced vibration when cutting metal, the orbit feature must be turned off.)

The teeth on jigsaw blades usually point up to help pull the tool toward the work on each upstroke. This also tends to spew sawdust over the cut line and splinter the surface. Most saws now have a built-in blower to keep the line clear, but when cutting something expensive like hardwood paneling, a few anti-splintering precautions should be taken. Some jigsaws come with a small plastic insert that surrounds the blade closely where it enters the shoe, helping to hold wood fibers in place. Another trick: Tom often uses a metal-cutting blade to cut wood. "The tiny teeth reduce splintering," he says. "You can also score the cut line with a razor knife as long as you remember to cut on the waste side of the line." In any case, try a test cut on scrap first.

Other helpful tips: Ease the saw more slowly into a cut, turn off the orbit feature, cut with the wood's good side facedown or swap a dull blade for a sharp one. Even then, what works on pine might mangle maple. To get the most out of a jigsaw, the trick is to hit on just the right combination of variables: blade aggressiveness, downward and forward pressure, degree of orbit and stroke rate. Or, as Tom says simply, "whatever works."

TILTING BASE: Enables the saw to make beveled cuts. Tom tilts it just a few degrees when making scribing cuts.

« The teeth on jigsaw blades usually point up to help pull the tool toward the work on each upstroke. »

This 3-inch blade cuts particleboard, plywood and similar sheet materials. A longer blade would be wasted on the thin panels. (12 tpi)

A high-speed steel blade cuts metal and makes smooth cuts in wood. It's somewhat less expensive and less durable than a bimetal blade. (14 tpi)

Particularly good for use in cordless jigsaws, this thin-kerf metal-cutting blade requires less power during a cut than thicker blades. (24 tpi)

Scroll-cut blades have narrow bodies for smooth cuts and tight turns in wood. They're good for intricate work but shouldn't be overworked. (20 tpi)

[**mitersaws**]

ONE MEASURE OF A GOOD CAR-penter is whether he can marry two pieces of wood trim so tightly around a corner that they look as if they grew that way. To achieve such precision in years past, a trim carpenter would lug around a miter box with a stiff, fine-toothed backsaw locked into movable guides. Tom Silva cut his first miters and bevels on this deceptively simple tool, which demands patience, a keen eye and an exquisite touch to keep the saw's blade on track.

Now when Tom cuts trim, he reaches for his power miter saw. With its blade spinning up to 5,000 rpm, the saw screams through wood, leaving glass-smooth, laser-straight cuts that would be impossible even with a perfectly tuned miter box. This speed also makes it easy to shave whiskers off molding to make it fit perfectly on imperfect walls. Go back to a miter box? "Never!" Tom says.

The first power miter boxes (called chop saws for their slashing, downward-cutting motion) came out in the early 1970s. Next came the compound miter saw, which allowed the blade and motor to flop to one side. In a single pass, it could cut the compound angle—a miter on a bevel—which is a prerequisite for seamless crown molding. When Hitachi mated a compound miter saw to a radial-arm saw, it created the first sliding compound miter saw. The tool was a carpenter's dream: The motor could pivot up, down and sideways as it slid back and forth on two gleaming steel rails. This power-tool equivalent of a Veg-o-matic

could crosscut shelving boards, compound-cut crown, plow dadoes of any width and carve enough kerfs across plywood facing to make it bend like rubber. The tool warmed the heart of anyone with a penchant for precision and lots of wood to crosscut, including trim carpenters, siding contractors and deck builders.

Miter saws are classified by their blade diameters; most range from 6½ to 12 inches. Smaller saws are easier to tote and can fit in a

to prevent
the blade from shooting small wood pieces out the back of the saw, Tom attaches scrap plywood to the fence so that nothing but the blade can get past.

Sliding compound miter saws mate the wide-board cutting ability of a radial-arm saw to the portability of a contractor's chop saw—and have nearly rendered both obsolete. Expensive, yes, but if it's versatility you need, this is the machine.

car trunk, but Tom says, "If I had my choice, I'd always take a 12-inch saw." He gets smoother cuts with more teeth in the wood, and the extra cutting depth lets him muscle through 4x6s. Sliding saws do need space aft for their slides—some as much as 24 inches behind the fence. That's why you won't see one in Norm Abram's workshop; his counter-tops aren't wide enough. And he doesn't like the way some compound miter saws have a large gap in the fence right behind the blade. This gap accommodates generous miter and bevel angles but lets short offcuts zoom through and sometimes ricochet off the back. Tom agrees: "If you're slicing off a small piece of trim to use as a mitered return, you'll have to hunt through the sawdust to find it." Some

TABLE: Supports workpiece.

BLADE GUARDS

MITER LOCK: Holds the saw at a precise miter angle.

SLIDE LOCK: Prevents saw from sliding when carried.

RAIL: Enables a motor to slide forward and back; this saw has two, others have one.

BEVEL LOCK: Holds the saw at a precise bevel angle.

FENCE: Workpiece must rest against fence during cuts.

[miter saws]

One or two gleaming rails found near the back of the saw distinguish slide-compound miter saws from similar but less-versatile machines. On a standard miter saw, you'll find a simple up-and-down pivot instead; on a compound miter saw you'll find a pivot and a rotating base.

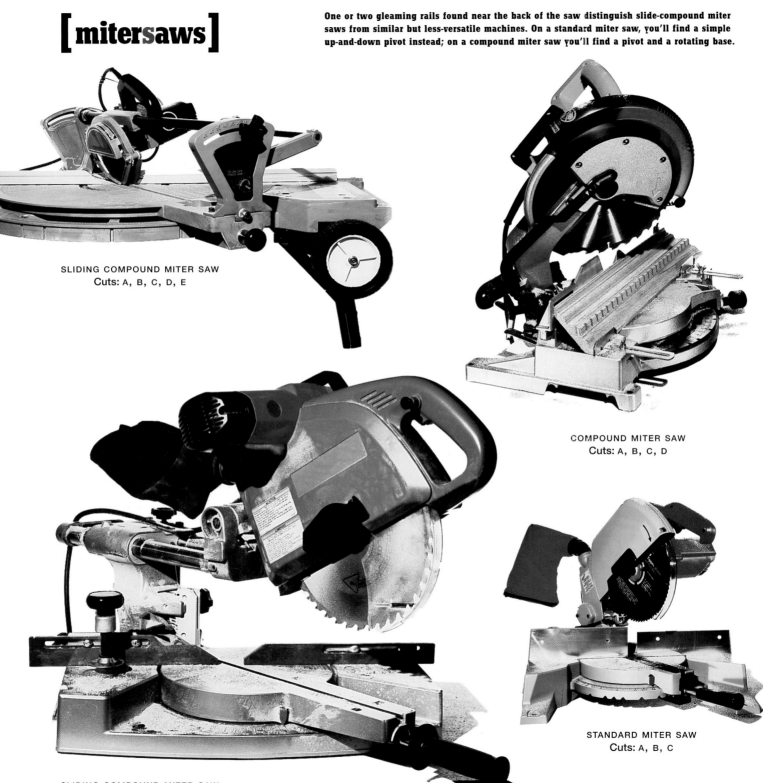

SLIDING COMPOUND MITER SAW
Cuts: A, B, C, D, E

COMPOUND MITER SAW
Cuts: A, B, C, D

SLIDING COMPOUND MITER SAW
Cuts: A, B, C, D, E

STANDARD MITER SAW
Cuts: A, B, C

saws have adjustable fences or sliding fence liners that can close this gap.

Tom prefers saws with a range of miter settings greater than 45 degrees—even an extra 5 degrees helps when trying to fit trim to a corner that isn't quite square. Long, floppy trim has to be supported during a cut or else the end being cut may lift and bind against the moving blade. At best, wood may be damaged; at worst, fingers could be severed. Blade

guards and automatic blade brakes help protect careless hands. A number of ingenious portable stock supports are available, but stacked 2x6 blocks will do if the saw is on the floor. Tom's knees prefer another solution: a sturdy, wheeled cart with adjustable rollers on each end. If there's trim to be done, you'll find him at his cart in a gathering cloud of sawdust, with his right arm pumping back and forth like an old-time miter-box pro.

Crosscut

Miter

Bevel

Compound Miter

Dado

* * *

MITER-SAW BLADES

NOT ALL CIRCULAR BLADES ARE CREATED EQUAL. THOSE FOR TABLE saws and portable circular saws have to crosscut and rip quickly through everything from green framing lumber to plywood. Their teeth lean forward in a compromise between speed and smoothness. Miter saws, however, dine on finer stuff—seasoned sticks of oak, pine and poplar—and they only crosscut. Each tooth of a miter-saw blade stands straight or reclines slightly. This is called zero, or negative, hook angle, and it makes ultrasmooth cuts.

More teeth mean smoother but slower cuts— and a costlier blade. Tom keeps only two blades for each of his miter saws. His 40-tooth model crosscuts inexpensive trim and the occasional stick of framing lumber with reasonable dispatch and minimal splintering. But for high-end crown, Tom likes 60 or 80 teeth, for a cut

so smooth it shines. Most saws come with a carbide-tipped alternate-tooth-bevel (ATB) blade, which crosscuts brilliantly but leaves a slightly ragged cut on dado bottoms. For the smoothest dadoes, the best blade is a carbide ATB-R model (left) with a flat raker tooth (A) to clean up after each pair of beveled teeth (B).

[nailguns]

SLAPPING TWO PIECES OF WOOD TOGETHER has for almost all of history been numbingly slow and laborious, a painfully primitive process of pounding on a steel spike with what amounts to a club. Modern hammers with brightly colored handles, contoured grips and polished heads haven't helped much. But deliverance arrived in 1968 with the invention of the pneumatic nail gun.

Tethered to compressors by lengths of high-pressure hose, the first models were clunky, expensive monsters, but they evolved into light, portable tools that pop nails into wood faster than most people can think. Best of all, nailers do so without denting wood, smashing thumbs or putting more money in the pockets of physical therapists. Tom Silva was one of the first residential carpenters to get one in the '70s. "I was watching an ad on TV, and I noticed a gun that shot nails being used in a factory," he recalls. He tracked down the manufacturer, who lent him a compressor and a couple of guns. "We were able to frame the last half of a three-story apartment complex in a third less time than we'd spent hand-nailing the first half," Tom says. Power nailers aren't merely faster; in many cases, they're better. A nail gun can punch a fastener into place in a single blistering shot. The wood, caught in a high-

FINISH NAILER: To insert or remove the fuel cell, lift a hatch. The battery (not shown) is parallel to the magazine. (5½ pounds)

STAPLER: Accepts 16-gauge wire staples from 1- to 2-inches long. (6⅓ pounds)

FRAMING NAILER: A grill and filter at the top of the motor housing strain out debris and airborne dirt. (7½ pounds)

« Gun-fired nails penetrate old, iron-hard framing that bends hammered nails. »

FINISH NAILER: 6⅓ pounds. The fuel cell on this type of gun slips into the handle. There is no battery.

tech ambush, can't wriggle or resist. Gun-fired nails penetrate old, iron-hard framing that bends hammered nails. There's no shaking; plaster stays put; wallboard won't pop. A day's work doesn't create more.

Until recently, every nail gun required an air compressor and a length of hose. A failure of any element and it was back to swinging clubs. The biggest aggravation, it turned out, was the hose. If it wasn't getting snagged—on a lumber pile, around a sawhorse leg—then it ended up an inch short of the target, like a too-short leash. Freedom came to nail guns in 1986, when the Paslode Corporation introduced a nail gun that functions without hose

or compressor. The gun is powered by internal combustion, just like the granddaddy of all portable machinery, the gasoline engine. Pulling the Paslode's trigger releases methyl-acetylene propadiene (MAPP) gas from a disposable fuel-cell cylinder and injects the gas into the combustion chamber. A spark detonates the mix and plunges a piston against the nail head, driving it home in one stroke.

At this point, Paslode makes its gaspowered guns in two versions: a framing nailer and a smaller model for finish work. The smaller gun gets about 2,500 shots per cylinder, the larger gun 1,200. Both versions operate similarly. Insert the fuel, snap on a

[nailguns]

how fast
*is a nail gun?
A lot faster than you
are. It punches
steel spikes or staples
through wood
in a single
800-mph strike.*

rechargeable battery, load a strip of collated nails and go. The 6-volt battery, which oper-ates the spark plug and a tiny fan, is good for about 4,000 shots between charges. With any nail gun, hoseless or otherwise, simply squeezing the trigger won't send steel spikes flying through the air. Before a gun will fire, you must press its nose firmly against a hard surface to release the safety. Pressing down the nose of the tool also kicks on the fan, which mixes air and fuel in the com-bustion chamber, then cools and clears the chamber after firing. Pushing down the nose takes more force than needed by a pneumatic nail gun—12 pounds versus 6. And the tool emits a firearm's crack rather than the pop of a pneumatic; wear ear protection. But the plastic housing makes the gun 1 to 2 pounds lighter than its metal pneumatic brethren, and it hooks easily onto a tool belt.

In 1997, Porter-Cable began manufac-turing gas nailers: a framer, two finish guns and a crown stapler for assembling cabinets and holding insulation. All use MAPP gas in a cylinder similar to the Paslode's, but they operate without fans, motors or batteries. A pressure-sensitive piezoelectric crystal, similar to that in a gas barbecue grill, generates the spark. The air and fuel are mixed and exhaust-ed as the tool is plunged, so cocking the gun requires 23 pounds of push. For a pro like Tom, extra effort lengthens a day. For a home owner who nails occasionally, it's a pick-up-and-go tool that cuts down on recharging time. The system requires little maintenance. The ignition should last for about 70,000 shots and can be replaced by the owner. It's time for a new one when you have to pull the trigger three or four times before it fires.

The Porter-Cable tools shoot two nails per second, the Paslodes shoot three, and pneumatic nailers can deliver five. Gas guns won't make Tom's trusty pneumatics obsolete, but if he has a small backyard job or some high nailing up on a roof, he'll grab one. "If we're running through a house, nailing up trim here and there, those guns are nice to have," he adds. "They're handy. No question about it."

CROWN STAPLES: From 1¼- to 2-inches long, they hold better than nails of like length. Used to fasten sheathing and subfloors.

FRAMING NAILS: D-shaped heads let them nest closely; codes restrict use in hurricane and earthquake zones.

FINISH NAILS: Blunt tips minimize splitting that often occurs near the end of wood trim. From ¾- to 2½-inches long.

COLLATING MATERIAL: Plastic gives D-head nails some flex. A shaft coating makes them easier to drive, harder to remove.

keep them dry, clean and cool

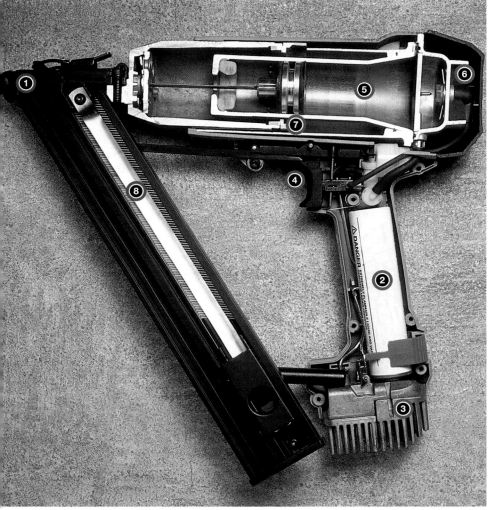

What's Up Inside: Pressing the nose of a gas nailer (1) against the work releases liquid MAPP from the fuel cell (2) to the fuel regulator (3), where the fuel mixes with air, changes from a liquid to a gas and is propelled into the fuel line. Pulling the trigger (4) sends the gas into the combustion chamber (5) and generates a spark at the plug (6). The gas ignites, driving the piston (7) onto the nail in the tool's magazine (8). Jammed fasteners are a frustrating reality of power nailing, but they're readily cleared in a gas nailer by flipping up the nose guard. (For safety, always remove the fuel cell or battery first.) A light blast of oil-free spray lubricant such as silicone clears grit and the bits of collating material that cause clogs. Tom (below) won't fire a nail gun unless his sight and hearing are protected.

GAS-POWERED NAILERS BREATHE AIR, SO MAKE SURE THEY GET PLENTY OF IT—CLEAN AND DRY. A SOFT FOAM FILTER BEHIND A GRILL KEEPS DIRT FROM HITCHING A RIDE ON INCOMING AIR FLOWING TO THE COMBUSTION CHAMBER (OR THE FAN, IN THE CASE OF THE PASLODE). IF THE FILTER CLOGS, THE GUN WON'T FIRE. TO CLEAN A FILTER, OPEN THE GRILL. ON PORTER-CABLE TOOLS, IT'S HELD BY FOUR SCREWS; THE PASLODE'S GRILL FLIPS UP. SHAKE OFF THE BIG CHUNKS OF GRIT, RINSE THE FILTER WITH DISH SOAP AND WATER, THEN SQUEEZE IT DRY BETWEEN PAPER TOWELS. STICK IT BACK IN AND GET TO WORK. DO THIS WHENEVER YOU REPLACE THE FUEL CELL. FILTERS WON'T STOP WATER, SO DON'T USE GAS NAILERS IN THE RAIN. IF A GUN GETS TOO COLD (BELOW 20-DEGREES FAHRENHEIT), ITS FUEL CELL WON'T MAINTAIN PROPER PRESSURE. IF A GUN GETS TOO HOT SITTING IN THE SUN, IT MAY CEASE FIRING OR FIRE INTERMITTENTLY. GUNS ARE ALSO ALTITUDE SENSITIVE, SO THEY MAY NOT WORK PROPERLY ABOVE 6,000 FEET.

[orbitsanders]

"DON'T SAND AGAINST THE GRAIN." IT'S THE FIRST WOODWORKING rule most people learn, whether they're using sheets of grit or a power sander. So you'll cringe the first time you sweep a random-orbit sander across the grain of a board. But as the surface smoothes with no sign of scratching, you'll see that this tool ignores the rule and gets away with it. As Norm Abram says, "It's not a magic tool, just a lot more forgiving than any other sander."

« As the pad spins in circles, an offset drive bearing causes it to move simultaneously in an elliptical orbit. »

A random-orbit sander incorporates two simultaneous actions: As the pad spins in circles, an offset drive bearing causes it to move in an elliptical orbit. The motion isn't truly random (the photo above shows how orderly it really is), but because the two motions overlap as you work, they reduce scratching across the grain and keep swirl marks to a minimum.

Versatility is another random-orbit hallmark. The tool can strip paint like a belt sander but is easier to control. It can finish like an orbital sander but without grain-direction worries. And because it can suck up and remove dust through holes in the pad, a random-orbit sander is great where ventilation is lousy. "This tool," says Norm, "is starting to dominate my sander collection."

The eccentric movement of the sanding pad enables Norm to disregard grain direction entirely, a real time-saver on furniture and cabinet projects. When sanding a dresser he built out of recycled antique pine, Norm hardly paused as he crossed the border onto its breadboard edge. Cabinet doors present a similar situation. The grain changes direction where stile meets rail, but a random-orbit sander zips over the intersection.

When it comes to finish sanding, a sander is only as good as your patience. The most common sanding mistake Norm sees is the failure to spend enough time with each grit. You have to start with coarse and earn your way up to fine, sanding thoroughly at each stage to avoid scratches at the end. Before changing grits, Norm slowly sweeps back and forth across the entire surface with over-lapping horizontal strokes, then recovers the territory with vertical strokes. "I start with 80 grit to strip a finish on solid wood," he says,

Three Amigos: 1. Palm-grip models are easy to hold against narrow surfaces such as cabinet face frames, and they maneuver like sports cars. Pads are 5 inches in diameter; most accept a vacuum attachment. 2. Right-angle models have gears that link their powerful motors to the sanding pad. This increases torque and reduces orbiting speed. The tool is a bit noisier (and more expensive) than the other sanders, but you can push it hard without slowing it down—a plus if you're stripping a finish or smoothing a glued-up surface. Norm prefers the greater coverage of 6-inch pads, but 5-inch pads are available. 3. An in-line sander is mechanically identical to a palm-grip model but includes a stronger motor, variable-speed control, handles and 5- or 6-inch pads.

[orbitsanders]

"otherwise the first step is 100 or 120 followed by 150. I stop there if the surface will be painted. If I'm staining, I go to 180 grit and then 220."

A random-orbit sander and silicon carbide sandpaper are ideal for taking scratches out of solid-surface countertops. The process generates extremely fine dust and a minute amount of styrene vapor, however, so a vacuum or a fitted, NIOSH-approved respirator is a must (see page 98).

Some in-line and palm-grip sanders will scuff wood. The pads start spinning as soon as the trigger is pulled, but the orbiting motion doesn't kick in until the tool is in full contact with the wood. In that moment of transition, the sander can leave an arc of scratches where it first touches down. Many sanders have features that minimize scuffing, but Norm still thinks it's best to start random orbit sanders while they're flat against the wood. Because random-orbits generate a lot of dust, most have a bag or canister to collect dust sucked through holes in the sanding pad; a vacuum hookup is even more efficient, so Norm hooks his to a shop vac that starts automatically when he turns on the sander. Dust collection suffers, however, if holes in the pad don't line up with those in the paper. Discs can have as few as five holes or as many as 16, so make sure that the ones you buy match your machine. The easiest way to ensure a match is to take an old disc along with you the next time you're out to purchase new ones.

One last tip: When using a sander and a shop vac, lift (don't drag) the vacuum hose over your work. As Norm learned the hard way, hose ribs can rasp away wood edges.

choosing sandpaper

THE RIGHT SANDPAPER IS CRUCIAL FOR TOP PERFORMANCE, BUT CHOOSING IT IS TRICKY. SANDING PADS ACCOMMODATE HOOK-AND-LOOP (VELCRO-TYPE) OR PRESSURE-SENSITIVE ADHESIVE (PSA) DISCS, BUT NOT BOTH. HOOK-AND LOOP DISCS CAN BE TAKEN OFF AND REATTACHED AS OFTEN AS NEEDED; THEY'RE THE BEST CHOICE IF YOU CHANGE GRITS FREQUENTLY. PSA DISCS ARE LESS EXPENSIVE, BUT YOU CAN'T REATTACH THEM. DISCS COME IN 5- AND 6-INCH SIZES TO MATCH THE PAD DIAMETER OF THE SANDER.

FOR PERFECT PLACEMENT EVERY TIME (WELL, ALMOST), NORM SIGHTS THROUGH THE PAPER'S HOLES AS HE PRESSES THE DISC INTO PLACE. THE SANDPAPER BACKING—WHAT THE GRIT STICKS TO—IS USUALLY PAPER. LIGHTWEIGHT BACKINGS ("A" WEIGHT) ARE BEST FOR FINISH SANDING; HEAVIER BACKINGS ("C" AND "D") ARE FOR HEAVY-DUTY STOCK REMOVAL OR SANDING HARD SURFACES. UNCOATED ALUMINUM OXIDE IS THE BEST ABRASIVE TO USE ON RAW WOOD. ON PAINTED OR SEALED WOOD, USE STEARATED ALUMINUM-OXIDE DISCS TO MINIMIZE CLOGGING.

* * *

PAD SANDERS

RANDOM-ORBIT SANDERS ARE CHAMPS for creating even, swirl-free surfaces, but for all-round sanding—fast cutting on large flat surfaces, smoothing rough wood and preparing wood for coats of paint or varnish—it's hard to beat an orbital or pad sander. The machine's wide base and gentle, easily controlled motion makes it good for jobs as diverse as smoothing plaster walls and sculpting Bondo-bolstered auto bodies. The smallest models, with petite square or rectangular pads, are light and maneuverable enough to run one-handed over most surfaces.

Unlike the multirotational rumba of a random-orbit sander, the pad sander dances in predictable "orbits" or circles. Sand soft pine with a coarse grit and you'll see the pad's motion in the hundreds of tiny spirals and corkscrews left on the wood's surface. But by using sandpaper in a graduated fashion from coarse to medium to fine, the surface can be smoothed quickly with minimal scratching—as long as you move the sander with, not against, the grain (you remember the rule, don't you?).

Following World War II, woodworkers had the meager sanding choice of a belt sander or doing the whole task by hand. In 1947 came the one-third sheet Sterling 1000, perhaps the first true orbital sander. The tool found immediate acceptance by woodworkers despite its unheard of price of $115. Other manufacturers eventually added half-sheet, quarter-sheet and sixth-sheet sanders to the genre, along with features such as dust extraction, electronic speed control, sound reduction and comfortable grips. If large panels are what you sand most, a half-sheet model is the way to go. If your primary task is smoothing trim or cabinetry, a quarter-sheet or smaller model will do just fine.

A sixth-sheet pad sander (top) can be maneuvered with one hand; its half-sheet cousin calls for two. Either way, be sure the paper-clamping device is easy to use; many aren't.

[**reciprocatingsaws**]

"IT CAN CUT OUT, NOTCH OUT OR remove, and as long as the plumber doesn't go after my framing with it, I love to have one on a job." That's Tom Silva describing reciprocating saws, brawny tools that have the lineage of a jigsaw and the attitude of a rottweiler. "I can't live without one during demolition," he adds. The saw is simple and relatively safe to use, and it's great for reaching the unreachable—wood or metal. Your first cut, though, might surprise you. If it seems like your arms are about to vibrate off, just hold the saw's shoe against the workpiece and push down a bit on the front of the boot; as the blade finally bites into wood, the saw will simmer down. Tamed.

The original "reciprocating-action saw" was the handsaw at the end of a carpenter's arm, but it tended to be slow and prone to muscle fatigue. In 1951, the Milwaukee Electric Tool Co. introduced the first portable electric reciprocating saw, tagged Sawzall for its versatility. Essentially a powerful in-line jigsaw, it weighed 6¾ pounds, produced 2,250 strokes per minute and cost all of $78.50. The Sawzall trade name has since become short-hand for any reciprocating saw, although at least six other brands are now on the market. The tool is a favorite of many tradespeople, including plumbers, electricians, demolition contractors and old-house remodelers.

Being an old-house guy, Tom is the sort who smiles when the walls are open and old wood, sawdust, pipe stubs and piles of stuff

When there's a roof to rip into (above) or a wall to remove, a recip saw can be more valuable than a hammer and pry bar. It's a two-handed power tool, however: The trigger hand controls speed and depth while the other guides the blade.

D-HANDLE: An enclosed grip protects the hand from the hazards of demoliton work.

TRIGGER SWITCH: Some saws have a variable-speed trigger; other saws have one or two speeds.

MOTOR HOUSING: May contain a switch that changes saw's speed.

ORBIT CONTROL SWITCH: Changes blade motion from straight (best for metal) to orbital (faster when cutting wood).

CORD PROTECTOR: Reduces stress where power cord enters tool.

BOOT: Rubberized coating dampens vibrations and provides a non-slip grip for one hand.

SHOE: Pivoting plate rides against material being cut to guide saw.

SAW BLADE: Some saws have a quick-change blade system that does not require a special tool.

A reciprocating saw can open a wall with ease, but Tom will tell you—rather emphatically—that you'd better be careful. He once sliced through six water pipes leading to second-floor radiators as he severed studs in the wall below. Wiring poses an equal hazard; always assume that something lurks beneath wall surfaces. Open a small hole, then peer into the wall cavity to investigate before launching a recip-saw attack. To prevent the wood lath in a plaster wall from vibrating loose, hold the saw at a shallow angle while cutting. Dust can be minimized by having a helper hold a vacuum nozzle near and slightly below the cut line.

[reciprocatingsaws]

are all over the place. That means hard work for his recip saws, though. "I've gone through a lot of 'em," he says—but when he has to replace one, Tom knows what he wants: variable speed controlled by a trigger. It gives more control over the cut, and, he says, "I really don't want to stop the saw to adjust its speed." He also likes dual orbital/straight cutting action. On the orbital setting, the blade moves up and down slightly as it goes back and forth, cutting through wood faster. On the straight setting, the blade moves back and forth only; that's better for cutting metal and making fine cuts in wood. Another feature that's nice is a quick-change blade clamp. Blades on many recip saws, including most of the old ones, are pinned to the saw's shaft with an Allen screw; if the screw doesn't get lost in the hurly-burly of demolition, the Allen wrench will. Tom likes the newer toolless systems that secure any blade with a quick twist of the locking collar.

When Tom cuts into walls (top), a shallow angle reduces the chance of damaging what's inside. To remove a floorboard (above), he plunge-cuts between board and support; the saw will slow when it hits the nail, then surge as it cuts through.

* * *

RECIPROCATING SAW BLADES

IT'S NOT UNUSUAL FOR TOM AND HIS CREW TO BLAZE THROUGH $150 worth of blades in a month; most are either 7-inch all-purpose blades or 12-inch rough-in blades. "I like the finer cut that the all-purpose blade gives on wood, especially plywood," he says, "but the other one cuts faster." He checks used blades for sharpness by pressing a thumb against the teeth: "You'll feel the sharp blades—toss the others." A blade gets hot in use, so don't grab one bare-handed: Wear gloves or let it cool before changing it.

choosing a blade

TOM FAVORS BIMETAL BLADES FOR MOST OF HIS WORK. FOR OPTIMAL PERFORMANCE, THEY HAVE FLEXIBLE SPRING-STEEL BODIES AND HARDENED TOOL-STEEL TEETH. THE COMBINATION LETS BIMETAL BLADES CUT THROUGH NAIL AFTER NAIL IN DEMOLITION WORK. SPRING-STEEL BLADES COST LESS BUT WON'T CUT MORE THAN A NAIL OR TWO WITHOUT BEING DAMAGED. IN ANY BLADE, TOOTH WEAR IS TYPICALLY GREATEST WITHIN AN INCH OR TWO OF THE SAW'S SHOE. TO GET MORE LIFE OUT OF A WORN BLADE, ADJUST THE SHOE SO A SLIGHTLY DIFFERENT PORTION OF THE BLADE GETS MORE OF THE ACTION. YOU CAN TURN A LONG, STIFF BLADE WITH LOCALIZED TOOTH WEAR INTO A HAND SAW FOR CUTTING HOLES IN DRYWALL: SIMPLY WRAP THE SHANK WITH DUCT TAPE TO MAKE A HANDLE.

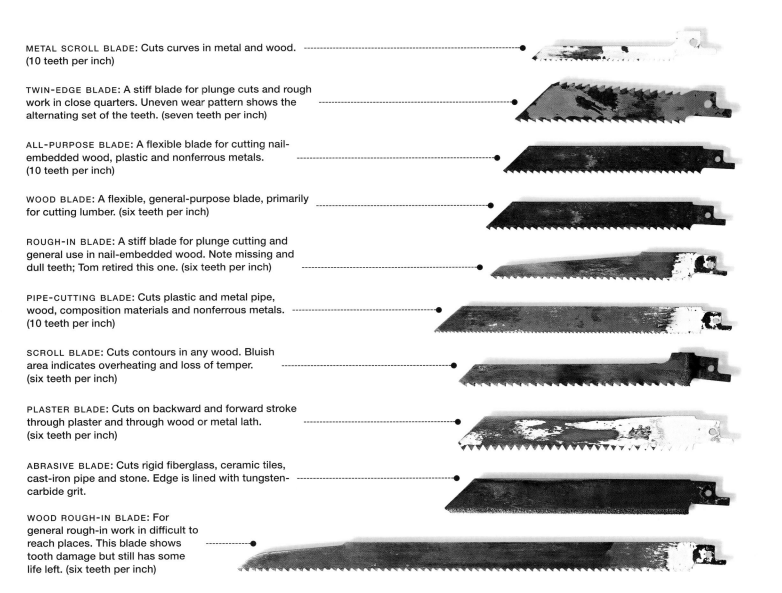

METAL SCROLL BLADE: Cuts curves in metal and wood. (10 teeth per inch)

TWIN-EDGE BLADE: A stiff blade for plunge cuts and rough work in close quarters. Uneven wear pattern shows the alternating set of the teeth. (seven teeth per inch)

ALL-PURPOSE BLADE: A flexible blade for cutting nail-embedded wood, plastic and nonferrous metals. (10 teeth per inch)

WOOD BLADE: A flexible, general-purpose blade, primarily for cutting lumber. (six teeth per inch)

ROUGH-IN BLADE: A stiff blade for plunge cutting and general use in nail-embedded wood. Note missing and dull teeth; Tom retired this one. (six teeth per inch)

PIPE-CUTTING BLADE: Cuts plastic and metal pipe, wood, composition materials and nonferrous metals. (10 teeth per inch)

SCROLL BLADE: Cuts contours in any wood. Bluish area indicates overheating and loss of temper. (six teeth per inch)

PLASTER BLADE: Cuts on backward and forward stroke through plaster and through wood or metal lath. (six teeth per inch)

ABRASIVE BLADE: Cuts rigid fiberglass, ceramic tiles, cast-iron pipe and stone. Edge is lined with tungsten-carbide grit.

WOOD ROUGH-IN BLADE: For general rough-in work in difficult to reach places. This blade shows tooth damage but still has some life left. (six teeth per inch)

[**routers**]

WOODWORKING CRAFTSMEN ONCE RELIED on an arsenal of wood planes to charm the corners off boards and coax curves out of straight stock, but Tom Silva does that and much more with an electric router. In his hands it shapes edges, cuts dovetails, plows grooves and sculpts the sinuous curves of custom molding profiles. It cuts away damaged wood, duplicates patterns, excavates hinge mortises and trims plastic laminate with utter precision. Though some woodworkers still prefer the long, fragrant shavings and quiet demeanor of classic hand planes, most depend on the can-do efficiency of a router. Tom's favorite type of router is a plunge router with a motor that moves up and down on spring-mounted posts, enabling the bit to be lowered—"plunged"—into the workpiece. The base of the tool stays flat on the workpiece at all times, making a plunge router easier to control and safer to use than standard routers. "I like my routers plain and simple," says Tom, but with eight in his stable, the standing joke at This Old House is that he never has to change a router bit—he just changes routers.

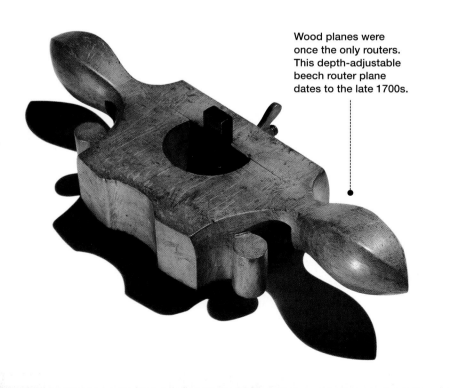

Wood planes were once the only routers. This depth-adjustable beech router plane dates to the late 1700s.

A router relies on speed, not strength, for it's cutting prowess. The faster the bit turns, the smoother the cut. Threaded on the end of a router's motor shaft is a collet that grips the bit's shank securely. Good thing, too, because a sharp chunk of steel spinning at 23,000 rpm would present a formidable wood-wrecking challenge if the collet ever let go.

Collets are classed by the largest size of bit shank they'll accommodate: ½-inch collets are typically found on high-powered, heavy-duty routers aimed at professionals, while ⅜- and ¼-inch collets are found on everything else. Half-inch bits are more expensive and not as easily available as other bits, but they're

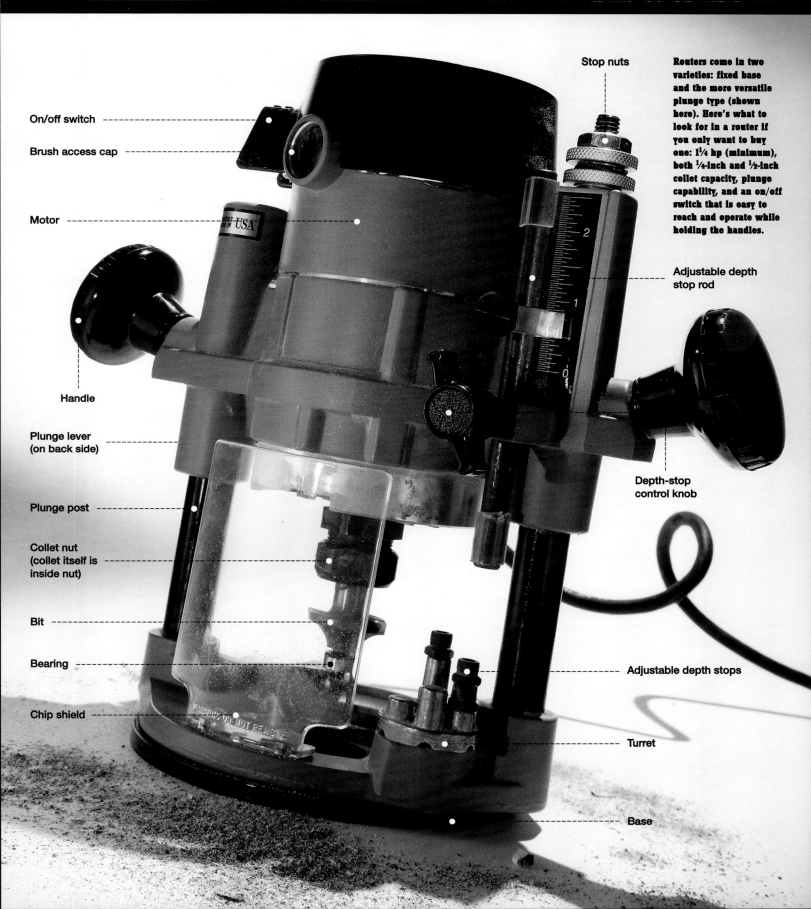

On/off switch

Brush access cap

Motor

Handle

Plunge lever
(on back side)

Plunge post

Collet nut
(collet itself is
inside nut)

Bit

Bearing

Chip shield

Stop nuts

Adjustable depth
stop rod

Depth-stop
control knob

Adjustable depth stops

Turret

Base

Routers come in two
varieties: fixed base
and the more versatile
plunge type (shown
here). Here's what to
look for in a router if
you only want to buy
one: 1¼ hp (minimum),
both ¼-inch and ½-inch
collet capacity, plunge
capability, and an on/off
switch that is easy to
reach and operate while
holding the handles.

[routers]

sturdier. Another factor in choosing a router is weight, because they range from Isetta-like 3½-pounders to 18-lb. Shermans. Weight means horsepower in the router world, so the trick is picking a router that's powerful enough to get the job done without giving your biceps a workout. "The one I use," says Tom, "depends on what I'm cutting." He might drag out a 3¼-hp beast to form the curves of a maple handrail, but a 1¼-hp router is quite suitable for beveling an edge or cutting mortises. Plenty of routers have even less power (and weight), but Tom figures that 1¼ hp is about the minimum worth having.

Like choosing a belt sander, choosing the right plunge router calls for some hands-on decision making: It's important to heft a router before committing to it, because handle configurations vary considerably, and so does balance. But from a safety standpoint, the two most crucial features are the on/off switch and the plunge-lock release lever. Depending on where they are, you'll find the router either a joy to use or a constant source of aggravation. Hold the router on a solid surface (unplugged and sans bit), then do the following with both hands on the tool: Turn on the switch, plunge the tool downward and then lock it in place with the plunge lever. Now release the lever, let the tool ride upward and then flip off the

TECHNIQUES

If You Don't Measure, Tom figures, you can't measure wrong (above). To cut the dado (a flat-bottomed groove) for a shelf standard, he first pushes down on his unplugged router until the bit just touches the wood. Then, keeping the router in this position, he sandwiches the standard between the depth-stop rod and a stop on the turret, then tightens the depth-stop knob.

Always Guide A Router if the bit doesn't have a pilot of its own. Tom often puts a metal straightedge to work (below), but a straight, flat board can work, too. Either way, the straightedge must be clamped to the work at both ends. Here Tom uses a mortise bit to cut a channel for a shelf standard. As he moves the router steadily forward, sawdust shoots backward and fills the newly cut channel as fast as he creates it.

Guiding A Router Is Critical, but there's more than one way to get the job done (above). Tom sometimes uses this adjustable fence when he has to make long cuts within a foot or so of edges. Its twin rails slip into guides on the router and can be tightened simply by turning down a couple of nuts. The fence rides against the edge of a board or panel, preventing the router from straying. It won't work, however, if cuts must be made in the middle of a panel.

router safety

RAZOR-SHARP EDGES AND WHIRLWIND SPEEDS CHEW THROUGH SEASONED MAPLE WITH EASE, SO IT'S NO SURPRISE THAT FLESH AND BONE DON'T STAND A CHANCE. THE FIRST STEP TOWARD ROUTER WISDOM, SAYS TOM, IS TO MOVE THE TOOL COUNTERCLOCKWISE AROUND AN OUTSIDE EDGE. THAT WAY THE CLOCKWISE-SPINNING BIT WILL BITE INTO THE WOOD INSTEAD OF CLAW ACROSS IT, A SITUATION THAT LEADS TO LOSS OF CONTROL. AT CORNERS, WHERE THE ROUTER'S BASE HAS THE LEAST SUPPORT, TOM SLOWS DOWN AND KEEPS ONE ROUTER HANDLE OVER THE WORKPIECE FOR IMPROVED CONTROL. WHATEVER THE SITUATION, HOWEVER, HE HOLDS THE TOOL FIRMLY WITH BOTH HANDS AND MAINTAINS A STEADY, BALANCED STANCE. "FEEL COMFORTABLE," HE SAYS, "BUT BE READY FOR ANYTHING."

ROUTERS SPRAY CHIPS TO THE FOUR CORNERS OF A SHOP, SO TOM INSISTS ON EYE AND HEARING PROTECTION. MOST ROUTERS HAVE A CHIP SHIELD THAT DEFLECTS SOME OF THE SPRAY, BUT ONLY FOOLS RELY ON IT FOR EYE PROTECTION. AND TO COMBAT THE NOTORIOUS WAIL OF A ROUTER, TOM PLUGS HIS EARS WITH COMPRESSIBLE FOAM PLUGS; EARMUFF-TYPE HEARING PROTECTORS ALSO WORK WELL AS LONG AS THEY FIT CORRECTLY.

« Rather than hog off the wood in one pass, Tom coaxes it off in two or three successively deeper passes. That's the beauty of a plunge router. »

switch. Try this routine with various routers until you find one that suits you.

Another feature Tom likes on a plunge router is adjustable depth stops. These slender posts sit atop a rotating turret and can be swung into position beneath the depth rod of a router, letting Tom make repetitive plunge cuts at three different depths. That's how small routers can do big work: Rather than hog off the wood in one pass, Tom coaxes it off in two or three successively deeper passes.

Whatever the features, however, Tom offers a simple description of his plunge router: "It's a tool I couldn't do without."

the first *powered routers date to about 1872. They worked fine—as long as the operator kept pedaling. Connected to a geared metal shaft, a foot crank spun bits at speeds up to 2,500 rpm.*

[routers]

* * *

ROUTER BITS

BITS, MORE THAN ANY ROUTER FEATURE, ARE WHAT MAKE THE TOOL so versatile. These whirling chunks of steel come in a wondrous variety of profiles and sizes, but unless they're sharp and free of nicked edges, they won't cut right—or safely. Carbide bits keep a sharp edge longer than inexpensive high-speed steel bits. But test the cutting edge of any bit before each use by brushing it lightly across your fingernail; if it doesn't grab, it's dull. To protect his bits from damage, Tom sticks them shank-first into a wood block drilled with suitably spaced holes. Clean bits work best. Remove accumulated pitch and grime with oven cleaner and a toothbrush, then relubricate the pilot bearing, if the bit has one, with sewing-machine oil.

V-GROOVE: Sometimes called a veining bit, it's used to letter or decorate. Two flutes (cutting edges) are angled at 60 , 90 or 120 degrees. Changing cutting depth widens or narrows the groove.

DOVETAIL: Often used with a template to make drawers, but Tom uses his "a lot" for other joinery. The bit shouldn't be withdrawn from a cut until it exits the board. Comes in various sizes and angles.

MORTISE: Best for routing the recesses (mortises) for hinges and hardware, this bit makes perfectly flat cuts. Cutter diameters range up to 1¼ inches. It's a poor choice for plunge cuts, however.

ROUND-NOSE: Also called a core box bit, it can cut the orderly flutes of a classical column. Tom has also used his to make the chalk rail for a child's chalkboard. Depth of cut affects groove width.

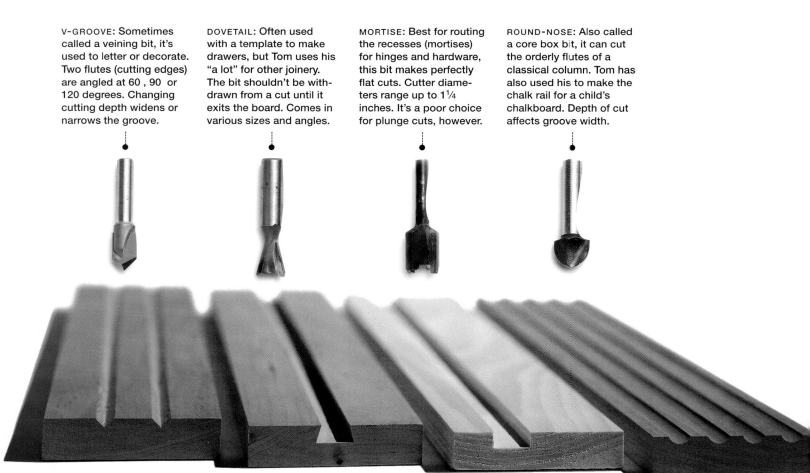

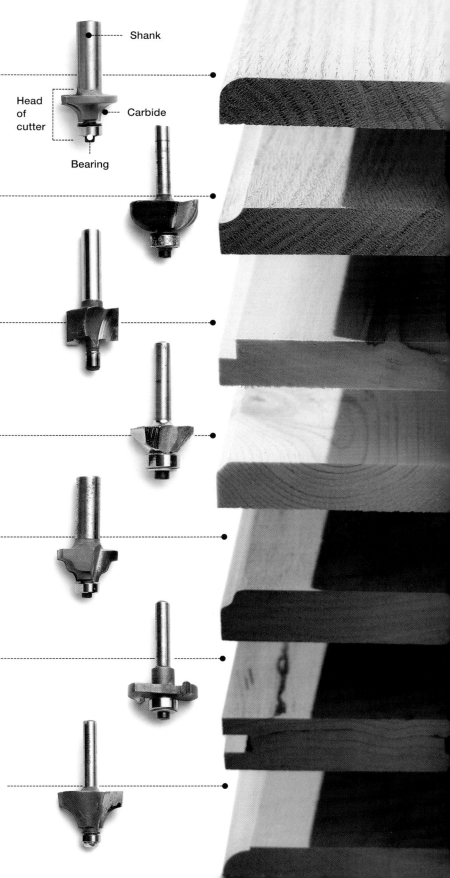

ROUNDOVER BIT: A bearing on any bit prevents it from taking too big a bite and keeps the cut on the edge of the wood. This bit has a roller bearing (most effective) and carbide cutting edges for supersmooth cuts. Use a roundover bit to ease any edge. Fitted with a smaller bearing, it becomes a beading bit (see below).

Shank

Head of cutter

Carbide

Bearing

COVE BIT: A cove is like a round-nose with a bearing. When cutting a deep cove, especially in hardwood, best results come with several successively deeper passes; this is where a plunge router excells. Tom once used his cove bit to shape the maple edge of a kitchen countertop—scooping out the wood and the plastic laminate in a single pass.

RABBET BIT: This bit cuts a lip (rabbet) into the edges of boards. Use it on the back edges of a cabinet to inset a plywood panel, create lipped cabinet doors or turn old boards into shiplap paneling. The bit shown here has a pilot bearing—a fixed pin that rides against the wood. It works like a roller bearing, though too much sideways pressure will friction-scorch the wood.

CHAMFER BIT: Tom calls it a "great finishing-of bit." Like a cove, it can detail the edge of a laminate countertop or dress up the edges of a post. Chamfer bits from $11\frac{1}{4}$ degrees to 45 degrees are available.

OGEE BIT: Ogees usually feature a mix of curves and flats that make them look like a cove bit and a beading bit in one. Tom's unusual ogee has an especially sinuous profile. "We make a great little detail on window muntins with this bit," he says.

SLOT CUTTER: Here's the bit for making tongue-and-groove flooring or spline joints, in which a narrow strip of wood (spline) is inserted between two edge-slotted boards. Tom's trick for centering the cut without measuring: eyeball the middle of the board, make one cut on the edge of an equally thick scrap board, then flip the board over and make another cut from the other side. Adjust bit height until two passes cut in the same place.

BEADING BIT: The bearing on this bit stops just short of the cutting edge, which leaves a reveal, or tiny lip, below the radiused bead. Adjust the height of the bit to cut a matching reveal above the bead —test cuts are mandatory. Cut a bead (also called an ovolo) where you want to set off an edge—a shelf, a baseboard, a window ledge.

[safetygear]

STANDARD SAFETY GOGGLES ARE sweaty and geeky looking, so they're not worn as often as they should be. Is that why there are so many work-related eye injuries in the United States? Perhaps we need a style fix, some not-your-father's-goggles safety glasses. Rarely found at your local hardware store, the good ones come from safety catalogs—whichever model you pick, be sure they are marked "Z87" (thus complying with OSHA impact standards).

A face shield (top) offers full-face protection from spraying sawdust. This one has a padded brow strap. The circular ports on indirectly vented goggles (above) admit air but impede splashed liquids; some offer impact protection as well.

Options shown include wraparounds, designs with brow bars and molded side shields, aviator types and designs that fit over your prescription glasses. Tom Silva sometimes wears safety glasses with a yellowish tint to the lenses. "They're nice for working inside where it's not well lit," he says. "Seems like they brighten it up a bit." And take note: The glasses at right are for impact hazard only; for splash or dust protection, goggles are better.

You'll find a goggle of choices if glasses won't suit. Two basic types are readily available. Standard goggles are the steamy standbys that show up in hardware stores. Enclosing the eye area makes good sense for splash protection and keeps flying shards and airborne dust from settling behind the lenses, but they fog up with distressing frequency. Ventilated goggles are the next step up. They're more expensive but are fog resistant. In either case, look for housings that are pliable, not stiff and uncomfortable.

A face shield deflects sawdust, but it's no substitute for impact-resistant safety glasses. Wear both for the best protection.

WRAP GLASSES: Curved lenses fit close to the face and offer good peripheral vision.

TINTED VIEW: Molded side shields are tinted to reduce glare. This pair includes a brow bar.

JAZZ GLASSES: Clear side shields permit an unob-structed view while blocking debris.

OVER VIEW: A contoured brow bar protects eyes from falling particles. Fits over prescription glasses.

STEALTH GLASSES: Aviator-style safety glasses masquerade as regular glasses but protect better.

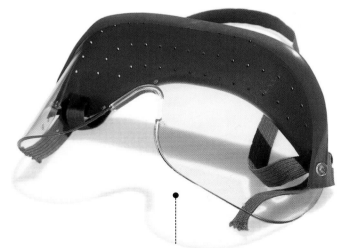

VISOR VIEW: Goggles with an integral visor reduce eye strain caused by strong overhead lighting.

[safetygear]

FOAM INSERTS: Self-adjusting foam expands slowly to fit the ear canal.

EVER READY: Pliable flanges with a neck strap adjust to an ear's contours.

DEEP EAR: A plug that's slightly longer than others fits some people better.

CYLIND-EAR: Triple-flanged plugs are reusable and are easy to remove. Disposable foam cylinders expand to seal the ear canal.

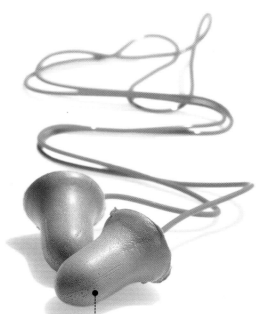

EAR BELLS: Flared ends make removal easier. Soil-resistant skin.

EAR CAPS: Soft foam caps cover the ear canal without requiring insertion.

* * *

WE'RE LOATH TO ADMIT IT, BUT OUR DAYS OF ENJOYING EAR-SPLITTING power tools (not to mention rip-roaring rock concerts) are over. What we seek most is blessed silence. And here's how we find it: Earmuffs may be hot and bulky and get in the way of hats and glasses, but Norm Abram and Tom Silva prefer them because they're typically better at blocking sound than other types of hearing protection. Foam or plastic inserts are small, light and offer good hearing protection, but they're easy to lose (a string connector helps).

Molded-plastic earplugs offer hearing protection that's comparable to the squishy-foam variety; some people find them easier to insert too. *This Old House* host Steve Thomas keeps his earplugs in an old film canister in his tool belt. Semi-inserts don't protect as well as other varieties because they can't be fully inserted, but they're easy to pop on and off, and hang around your neck when you don't need them. Prices range from less than a dollar for foam inserts to $20 or so for earmuffs.

It can be a daunting task to select the right plug or muff from among the many shapes, sizes and types on the market. Finding one that's comfortable and convenient is the first step—and a crucial one—because you probably won't wear a hearing protector that you don't like. After that, compare the effectiveness of various products by checking their noise reduction rating (NRR). The NRR is measured in decibels (dB), so the bigger the number, the greater the noise reduction. It's common to find products ranging from NRR: 17dB to NRR: 30dB. Note: An earmuff won't necessarily rate higher than a earplug.

Earmuffs (left) and semi-insertable earplugs (right) are easy to don and less likely than earplugs to get lost when you doff them—they just hang around your neck until needed. For the best comfort and a proper fit, earmuffs should have an adjustable headband with pivoting ear-cup connections and pliable ear cushions.

[safetygear]

* * *

DUST MASKS AND RESPIRATORS

IT SOMETIMES SEEMS THAT OUR WORLD IS OUT TO GET US. SAWDUST, especially from beech and oak, has been linked to nasal cancer among furniture and cabinetmakers (a little sawdust is one thing; breathing it every day is quite another). Asbestos fibers, so thin that they settle deep inside the lungs, can cause cancer, and scientists suspect that any material of the same length and width—such as shreds of fiberglass insulation—may do the same.

pesticides?

A "pesticide" respirator won't protect against fumigants or even all pesticides. Check with the manufacturer to determine if the mask you use defends against the hazards you face.

Less well known is the sometimes fatal disease called silicosis that can be caused by dry-sawing cement or simply by sanding drywall joint compound.

Steve Thomas, like many people, used to cut, sand and paint with little thought about his lungs. Then he realized he had become allergic to all sorts of things: polyester resins; cedar, redwood and iroko sawdust; house paint. Even latex paint causes his throat to close up and his lungs to ache. So now he uses a respirator—not a flimsy dust mask but a silicone half-face respirator that accepts high-efficiency particulate air-purifying (HEPA) filters—for protection against dust and fumes. A respirator works by forcing the air you breathe to pass through filters or cartridges, or a combination of the two. Filters, which trap particles in a nonwoven fiber net, are rated by the size and number of particles that pass through. A HEPA rating is best; a dust/mist rating isn't as good. Replace filters when breathing becomes difficult. Be especially cautious if you have chronic health problems or are working in close quarters.

To provide defense against gases and vapors, most cartridges work by trapping contaminants in materials called sorbents. Cartridges work only for specific contaminants, however, and they wear out, sometimes even when not in use. If you smell what you're using or feel dizzy, get fresh air and replace the cartridge. If the problem recurs quickly, concentrations are too high for the mask.

Respirators, though, are just one way to prevent respiratory problems. First consider safer alternatives. Work outside if possible; indoors, open a window and set a fan in an opposite doorway, blowing toward you. Stand between the fan and your work so you stay in fresh air. Another approach: connect your power tools to a shop vacuum.

Disposable Respirator: Avoid throw-away single-band masks labeled "comfort mask" or "for nuisance dusts." Instead, go for one that's government tested (look for the NIOSH label) and has two rubber bands for a good seal (critical to a mask's performance). Some have a HEPA rating and an exhalation valve; some fold flat. **Air-Purifying Respirator:** A half-mask is suitable for most home jobs. A full-face model also protects eyes. Most have replaceable filters and cartridges. **Powered Air Purifier:** A motorized belt pack delivers filtered air to the face for easier breathing. This one works with trimmed beards; full hoods are also available. **Air-Supplying Respirator:** When cartridges can't work, one option is to connect to an outside air tank that is good for 30 to 60 minutes.

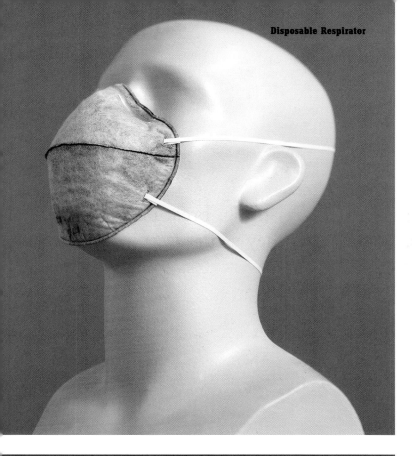

Disposable Respirator

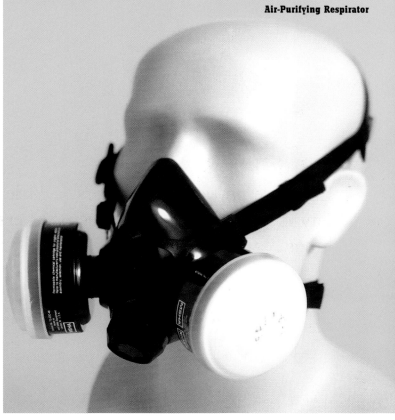

Air-Purifying Respirator

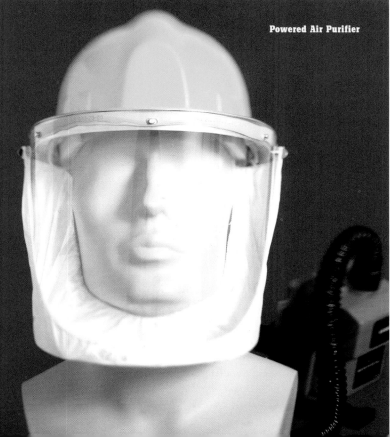

Powered Air Purifier

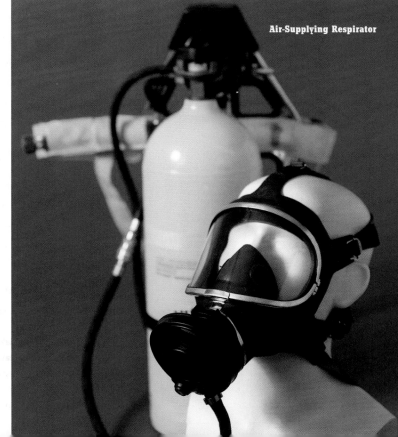

Air-Supplying Respirator

[studguns]

THE WAIL OF A CIRCULAR SAW AND THE steady rumble of a concrete truck have long been signature sounds of construction. Here's a new one: the whip-crack of steel being shot into concrete. The device at work is a "powder actuated fastener tool"—most workmen call it a stud gun. Tom Silva calls it invaluable.

There's no faster way to join wood to concrete or steel, he says. Tom uses his stud gun to nail framed walls or flooring sleepers to concrete floors, to secure wood nailers to steel support beams and to fasten furring strips to masonry-block walls. For finishing off a basement, he says, "Nothing beats 'em." The gunpowder charge, known as the load, determines how deep a pin will go. Loads, like the guns themselves, come in calibers of .22, .25 and .27. Pins also come in a variety of diameters, lengths and styles, depending on the job they need to do. Most are made of heat-treated, high-carbon steel, which will rust if it gets damp. Where corrosion could be a problem, use stainless-steel pins.

Even with all that firepower behind it, there's no guarantee a pin will penetrate. Concrete varies in density—old concrete is

SPALL GUARD: Optional steel collar prevents chipping when pin is fired into concrete.

MUZZLE: Guides ram to its target.

FASTENER: Can be a hardened-steel pin (shown) or a threaded stud. Plastic collar (in red) centers fastener in the barrel. Never use fasteners with damaged collars.

« It works like a miniature pile driver:

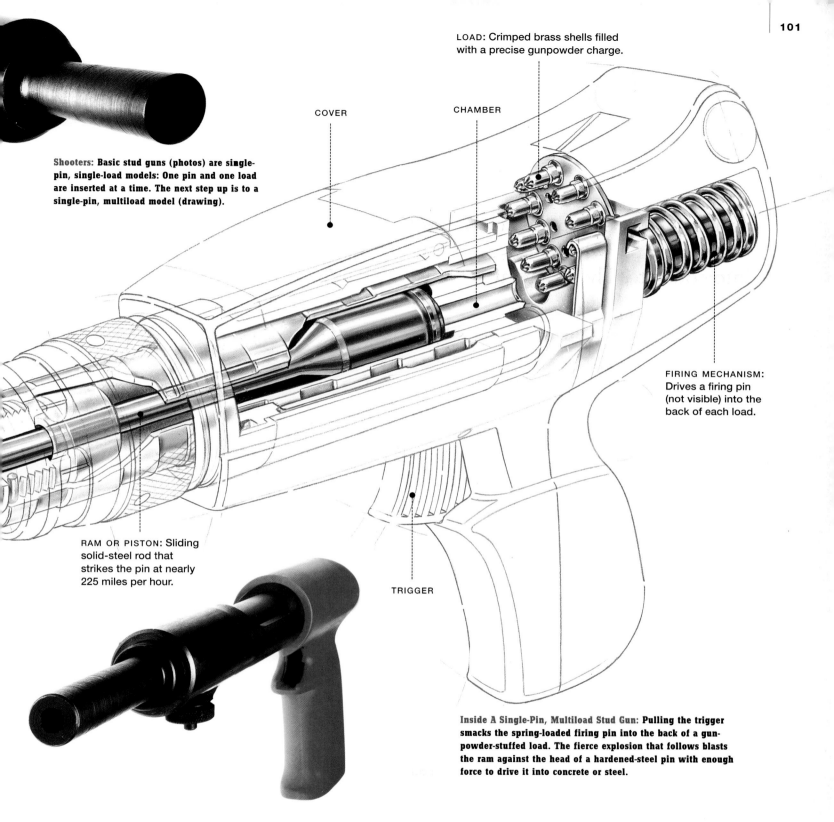

LOAD: Crimped brass shells filled with a precise gunpowder charge.

COVER

CHAMBER

Shooters: Basic stud guns (photos) are single-pin, single-load models: One pin and one load are inserted at a time. The next step up is to a single-pin, multiload model (drawing).

FIRING MECHANISM: Drives a firing pin (not visible) into the back of each load.

RAM OR PISTON: Sliding solid-steel rod that strikes the pin at nearly 225 miles per hour.

TRIGGER

Inside A Single-Pin, Multiload Stud Gun: Pulling the trigger smacks the spring-loaded firing pin into the back of a gunpowder-stuffed load. The fierce explosion that follows blasts the ram against the head of a hardened-steel pin with enough force to drive it into concrete or steel.

A powerful charge propels a ram against a hardened nail. »

[studguns]

FASTEN RIGHT: Pins (on left) are the standard fastener. Studs (red collar) have a threaded top to accept nuts. Pin clips secure conduit.

PIN ULTIMATE: Collated pins mean few reloadings between shots. As one pin is blasted home, the next slips into place.

LOAD ARRANGER: Individual loads stuck in a plastic collating strip speed the firing process by reducing the need to stop and reload.

ROOF PAL: These two-part plastic fasteners pin acres of rubber roof membrane to the broad, flat roofs of commercial buildings.

ON SOME OLDER STYLES OF STUD GUNS, THE POWDER CHARGE DROVE THE PIN DIRECTLY, BUT INJURIES MOUNTED AS THESE HIGH-VELOCITY GUNS SENT FASTENERS RICOCHETING OFF THE BASE MATERIAL OR THROUGH FLOORS AND HOLLOW WALLS. MANUFACTURERS STOPPED MAKING THE GUNS AND REPLACEMENT PARTS IN THE EARLY 1990S, AND NOW THE ONLY STUD GUNS SOLD LEGALLY ARE THE LOW-VELOCITY KIND—SLIGHTLY LESS EFFECTIVE BUT A GREAT DEAL SAFER.

EVEN WITH LOW-VELOCITY GUNS, IT'S CRUCIAL TO CLEAR THE AREA IN THE LINE OF FIRE, AS WELL AS AREAS ON THE OTHER SIDE OF A WALL OR FLOOR. HEARING PROTECTION IS ESSENTIAL, ESPECIALLY IN ENCLOSED AREAS. "THE SOUND IS WICKED," SAYS TOM. ALSO GET A GOOD PAIR OF Z87.1 (ANSI IMPACT RATED), SCRATCH-RESISTANT SAFETY GLASSES WITH SIDE SHIELDS TO STOP ERRANT PINS OR RICOCHETING BITS OF COLLAR.

PERIODIC MAINTENANCE IS CRUCIAL. A MODULAR DESIGN ALLOWS QUICK DISASSEMBLY, SO MOST GUNS CAN BE CLEANED AND SERVICED WITH MINIMAL EFFORT. FREQUENT CLEANING WITH A STIFF BRUSH AND A RAG MOISTENED IN A SOLVENT-BASED CLEANING FLUID REMOVES THE BLACK-GRAY POWDER RESIDUE THAT COLLECTS ON INTERNAL PARTS.

PARADOXICALLY, A STUD GUN REQUIRES LESS SKILL THAN A HAMMER SWING, BUT IT'S THE ONLY JOB-SITE TOOL THAT NEEDS AN OPERATING LICENSE. "YOU CAN'T LET JUST ANYONE USE ONE," CAUTIONS TOM. OSHA ENFORCES LICENSING FOR CON-TRACTORS BUT NOT FOR HOMEOWNERS. IF YOU RENT OR BUY A STUD GUN, HAVE SOMEONE THOROUGHLY EXPLAIN HOW TO USE THE TOOL. INSIST ON GETTING AN INSTRUCTION MANUAL. READ IT.

ask questions first, shoot later

harder than new, for example—and it's laden with stone aggregate that sometimes stops pins. Steel is also unpredictable. Tom never knows if the I-beam he's firing into is stewed from scrap bolts (soft) or Buick bumpers (hard). He usually test-shoots a couple of pins, starting with the lightest load he thinks will work, before he settles on a charge that doesn't bend the pin or send it too deep. In suspect surfaces, do a punch test first by hitting a pin with a couple of moderate hammer blows. If the pin's tip blunts, the material is probably too hard to shoot into. If the material cracks or chips, it's too brittle.

Once Tom matches a suitable pin and charge to the substrate, he can shoot as quickly as he can load. He just slips a pin into the barrel, holds the gun perpendicular to the surface, presses down hard with both hands (to cock the trigger) and fires—no drilling, no dust, no sweat.

Tom first used a powder-actuated tool more than 20 years ago, when his dad was running crews. "We'd put one pin and one shot into a thing that looked like a bicycle handgrip with a mushroom top, and I'd just whack it once with a small sledge." Later models replaced the sledge with a trigger-activated firing mechanism, and the modern stud gun was born. Sledge-driven models are still available, however; their low cost suits small projects or intermittent use.

Testing a new stud gun, Tom once fired repeatedly into a steel-beam offcut, which soon looked like the hapless patient of a construction acupuncturist. "Yep," he announced, "I think this will do just fine."

a perfect shot *in steel is easy to recognize. The pin should penetrate just past the taper of its point. Anything more stresses the pin and adds nothing to its withdrawal strength.*

Multishooter: This multipin and multiload model has a magazine that feeds collated pins as a disk or a strip feeds loads.

***
CREDITS

AUTHORS: Mark Feirer (Belt Sanders, Bench Grinders, Biscuit Joiners, Chainsaws, Circular Saws, Cordless Drills, Detail Sanders, Drills, Jigsaws, Miter Saws, Orbit Sanders, Reciprocating Saws, Routers, Stud Guns), David Frane (Bandsaws), Jeanne Huber (Safety Gear), John Kelsey (Drill Bits), Curtis Rist (Electric Planes), Greg Rössel (Pad Sanders), Ken Textor (Extension Cords), Arne Waldstein (Nail Guns).

PHOTOGRAPHERS: Neil Brown, Jim Cooper, Anthony Cotsifas, Carlton Davis, Michael Grimm, Darrin Haddad, Spencer Jones, Keller & Keller, Joshua McHugh, Martin Mistretta, Erik Rank, Wayne Sorce, Ted & Debbie, Jeff Von Hoene, Mark Weiss, Joe Yutkins

ILLUSTRATIONS: Clancy Gibson, Bob Hambly, Tom Siebers

THIS OLD HOUSE BOOKS®
EDITOR: Mark Feirer
DESIGN DIRECTOR: Matthew Drace
ART DIRECTOR: Delgis Canahuate
PROJECT COORDINATOR: Miriam Silver
PRODUCTION DIRECTOR: Denise Clappi
ART ASSOCIATE: Matthew Bates
PRODUCTION ASSOCIATE: Duane Stapp
COPY EDITOR: Eric Page

PUBLISHER, BOOKS: Andrew McColough
VICE PRESIDENT, CONSUMER MARKETING: Greg Harris

SPECIAL THANKS TO: Norm Abram, Steve Thomas, Tom Silva, Richard Trethewey, Bruce Irving and Russell Morash at the show; Karen Johnson and Peter McGhee at WGBH; Stephen Petranek and Eric Thorkilsen at *This Old House* magazine; Anthony Wendling and Ray Galante at Applied Graphics Technology; and interns Nataly Kolesnikova and Nino Kartozia.

Funding for *This Old House* on public television is provided by State Farm Insurance Companies, Ace Hardware Corporation and The Minwax & Krylon Brands.

« It's hard work and lots of it that warrants the speed and accuracy of a power tool. »